COMMUNICATING FINANCIALS TO EXECUTIVES

COMMUNICATING FINANCIALS TO EXECUTIVES

ANDERS LIU-LINDBERG AND

CHRISTIAN FRANTZ HANSEN

WILEY

Copyright © 2025 by John Wiley & Sons Inc. All rights reserved, including rights for text and data mining and training of artificial intelligence technologies or similar technologies.

Published by John Wiley & Sons, Inc., Hoboken, New Jersey.
Published simultaneously in Canada.

No part of this publication may be reproduced, stored in a retrieval system, or transmitted in any form or by any means, electronic, mechanical, photocopying, recording, scanning, or otherwise, except as permitted under Section 107 or 108 of the 1976 United States Copyright Act, without either the prior written permission of the Publisher, or authorization through payment of the appropriate per-copy fee to the Copyright Clearance Center, Inc., 222 Rosewood Drive, Danvers, MA 01923, (978) 750-8400, fax (978) 750-4470, or on the web at www.copyright.com. Requests to the Publisher for permission should be addressed to the Permissions Department, John Wiley & Sons, Inc., 111 River Street, Hoboken, NJ 07030, (201) 748-6011, fax (201) 748-6008, or online at http://www.wiley.com/go/permission.

The manufacturer's authorized representative according to the EU General Product Safety Regulation is Wiley-VCH GmbH, Boschstr. 12, 69469 Weinheim, Germany, e-mail: Product_Safety@wiley.com.

Trademarks: Wiley and the Wiley logo are trademarks or registered trademarks of John Wiley & Sons, Inc. and/or its affiliates in the United States and other countries and may not be used without written permission. All other trademarks are the property of their respective owners. John Wiley & Sons, Inc. is not associated with any product or vendor mentioned in this book.

Limit of Liability/Disclaimer of Warranty: While the publisher and author have used their best efforts in preparing this book, they make no representations or warranties with respect to the accuracy or completeness of the contents of this book and specifically disclaim any implied warranties of merchantability or fitness for a particular purpose. No warranty may be created or extended by sales representatives or written sales materials. The advice and strategies contained herein may not be suitable for your situation. You should consult with a professional where appropriate. Further, readers should be aware that websites listed in this work may have changed or disappeared between when this work was written and when it is read. Neither the publisher nor authors shall be liable for any loss of profit or any other commercial damages, including but not limited to special, incidental, consequential, or other damages.

For general information on our other products and services or for technical support, please contact our Customer Care Department within the United States at (800) 762-2974, outside the United States at (317) 572-3993 or fax (317) 572-4002.

Wiley also publishes its books in a variety of electronic formats. Some content that appears in print may not be available in electronic formats. For more information about Wiley products, visit our web site at www.wiley.com.

Library of Congress Cataloging-in-Publication Data:

Names: Liu-Lindberg, Anders, author. | Hansen, Christian Frantz, author.
Title: Communicating financials to executives / Anders Liu-Lindberg and Christian Frantz Hansen.
Description: Hoboken, NJ : John Wiley & Sons, Inc., 2025. | Includes bibliographical references and index.
Identifiers: LCCN 2024062192 | ISBN 9781394292608 (paperback) | ISBN 9781394292639 (epub) | ISBN 9781394292622 (pdf)
Subjects: LCSH: Business enterprises—Finance. | Business communication.
Classification: LCC HG4026 .L652 2025 | DDC 658.15/12—dc23/eng/20250218
LC record available at https://lccn.loc.gov/2024062192

Cover image(s): © Portra/Getty Images
Cover design: Wiley

SKY10104961_050525

CONTENTS

AUTHOR BIOGRAPHIES	xi
PREFACE	
OUR EXPERIENCE WITH FINANCIAL COMMUNICATION	xiii
CHAPTER 1	
WHY FINANCIAL COMMUNICATION TO EXECUTIVES REQUIRES SPECIAL ATTENTION	1
The Pressure Is Mounting on Executives	3
Insight × Influence = Impact	4
The Purpose of Finance	7
The Value of Finance	10
The Intrinsic Motivation for Finance Professionals	12
The Job Is on the Line	14
All We Need Is a Framework for Financial Communication	15
CHAPTER 2	
THE STRUGGLES OF FINANCE PROFESSIONALS TO COMMUNICATE FINANCIALS	17
The Three Main Challenges	19
Sharing Too Many Details	21
Having No Consistent Structure	23
Making No Apparent Recommendations	26
Meet Sarah, a Senior Financial Analyst	28

CONTENTS

CHAPTER 3

FIVE STEPS FOR COMMUNICATING FINANCIALS
TO EXECUTIVES ... 31

Take a Customer-Centric Approach ... 33

From Data to Insights ... 36

Five Steps for Financial Communication to Executives ... 38

Info ... 39

Insights ... 41

Recommendation ... 42

Evidence ... 44

Action ... 46

Sarah Gets to Know Her Customers ... 47

CHAPTER 4

STEP 1: INFORMATION: WHAT IS THE FINANCIAL STATUS? ... 51

Define an Objective and Target Stakeholder ... 52

Consider Your Audience ... 55

Data Extraction: Access Relevant Data Sources ... 57

Data Preparation: Build on a Proper Foundation ... 59

Master Data Management ... 59

Data Cleaning ... 60

Chart of Accounts and Financial Statements ... 62

Data Analysis: Extracting Relevant Insights ... 63

Horizontal Analysis ... 64

Vertical Analysis ... 66

Variances and Deviations ... 69

Using Technology to Your Advantage ... 70

Data Selection: Present Only What Matters ... 72

Moving from Information to Insights ... 75

Sarah's Data Struggle ... 76

Contents

CHAPTER 5

STEP 2: INSIGHTS: WHAT ARE THE KEY ATTENTION POINTS?   79

What Is an Insight?   80

Cater to Your Audience   85

Empathy: Present Insights Relevant to Your Stakeholders   86

Verify Your Understanding   90

Acknowledge Personality Types   91

Types of Analytics   93

Tips on How to Communicate Your Insights   99

Tip 1: Golden Rule of Three   99

Tip 2: Curate Based on Criteria   101

Tip 3: Do not Just Summarize – Synthesize   104

Moving from Insights to Recommendations   106

Sarah Uncovers the Root Causes of Poor Revenue
Performance   108

CHAPTER 6

STEP 3: RESOLUTION: WHAT CAN WE DO ABOUT IT?   113

Distinguish Between Output and Outcome   115

Dare to Have an Opinion   118

Leverage Structured Problem-Solving   120

Define the Problem   121

Disaggregate the Problem   124

Design the Solution   128

Tips for Making a Recommendation   129

Prototype – Make Your Solution Visible   129

Present Options – There Is Never Just One Solution
Option   130

Anticipate Objections – Be Ready with a Reply   131

Supporting Your Recommendation with Arguments   132

Sarah Ideates Potential Solutions   132

vii

CONTENTS

CHAPTER 7

STEP 4: ARGUMENTATION: WHY IS THIS A GOOD IDEA?	137
The Difference Between Argument and Facts	138
Facts: The Foundation of Trust	138
Arguments: The Art of Persuasion	139
The Interplay of Facts and Arguments	140
The Magic Number of Three: Why Three Arguments Are Ideal	142
The Psychology Behind the Number Three	143
Three Arguments to Convince Management	144
Expanding the Definition of Facts Beyond Numbers	146
Expert Statements	146
Customer Testimonials	147
Industry Research	148
Integrating Non-Numerical Facts with Financial Data	149
The Importance of Selectivity	150
Why Selectivity Matters	150
How to Select the Right Three Arguments	151
From Argument to Decision	153
Sarah Backs Up Her Recommendation	153

CHAPTER 8

STEP 5: HOW DO WE GET STARTED?	157
Summarize and Ensure a Common Understanding	157
Anticipate Change Resistance	158
The SCARF Model – Sources of Change Resistance	159
Pave the Way Forward	163
Insist on a Decision: Turning Discussion into Action	166
Getting Started with the New Sales Channel	169
It's Time to Present	171

Contents

CHAPTER 9
CONSIDERATIONS ON DATA VISUALIZATIONS 175
Make It Easy to Decode Your Key Message 177
System 1 and System 2 Thinking 180
Designing for System 1: Presenting Insights Clearly and Effectively 181
Engaging System 2 When Necessary 182
Minimizing Cognitive Load 182
A Picture Is Worth a Thousand Words 183
The Split-Attention Effect 185
Pre-Attentive Attributes and Gestalt Principles 186
Pre-Attentive Attributes: Highlighting the Key Message Instantly 187
Gestalt Principles: Organizing Information for Better Understanding 188
Tips for Better Data Visualization 189
Tips for Great Slide Making 196
Place the Argument in the Header 198
Use Action Titles in the Header and Charts 198
Stick to One Key Message per Slide 198
Present Only Evidence Supporting the Argument (in the Header) on the Slide 199
State Your Sources 199
Use Call-Outs to Highlight Key Points 199
Use Colours to Make Charts Easy to Read 200
Use Large Readable Fonts 200

CHAPTER 10
HOW TO PREPARE THE PERFECT MANAGEMENT REPORT 201
Structuring Your Management Report 203
A Mock-Up of the Perfect Management Report 206

CONTENTS

CHAPTER 11
HOW FINANCE PROFESSIONALS BECOME EXCELLENT
COMMUNICATORS   217
Without Using SCQA   220
With the Use of SCQA   221
Business Cases   222
From Analysis to Presentation   223
One Size Does Not Fit All   226
Final Tips on Communication   228
    Before the meeting   228
    At the meeting   229
    After the meeting   230

CHAPTER 12
PRACTICAL STEPS TO START IMPROVING YOUR
COMMUNICATION SKILLS   233
Taking the First Steps   235
    Comparison and Feedback   235
    Ask Your Audience   236
    Prepare Your Mock-Up   236
    Implement and Continuous Improvement   237
The Next Steps   238
    Awareness   239
    Desire   239
    Knowledge   239
    Ability   240
    Reinforcement   240
From Steps to a New Company Culture   241
It Is Time to Get to Work   243

REFERENCES   245
INDEX   249

AUTHOR BIOGRAPHIES

Anders Liu-Lindberg and Christian Frantz Hansen are both partners at Business Partnering Institute. They have worked together for several years to help finance professionals elevate their insights, influence, and impact on decision-making and value creation.

They have worked with finance teams worldwide and see their daily challenges in creating impact. They have made it their mission to give them the help they need.

Anders Liu-Lindberg is the co-founder and Chief Commercial Officer at Business Partnering Institute and an official LinkedIn influencer with 400,000+ followers. He is also the co-author of the book *Create Value as a Finance Business Partner*.

Christian Frantz Hansen is the Chief Product Officer at Business Partnering Institute and a seasoned management consultant in the CFO space. For 10+ years, he has delivered tangible impact through Financial Planning and Analysis and Business Finance academies for global clients.

PREFACE: OUR EXPERIENCE WITH FINANCIAL COMMUNICATION

It was a cold January day in 2017 on a ship in the port of Rotterdam, which had been converted into a hotel and conference facility. Anders had gotten up at 3:30 am to fly in from Copenhagen to participate in a training program for finance business partners. Christian was already there as a part of the consulting team that delivered the training. It was the first time Anders and Christian met, and while they did not know it then, it was the start of a relationship that would lead to them eventually joining forces as partners at Business Partnering Institute.

Here, we help finance teams become more influential and business-oriented to create value. That was also the training topic in January 2017, where areas like influencing skills, problem-solving and structured communication were part of the agenda. Why had Anders' company decided to invest in elevating these skills in their finance business partners? It was because they did not have enough impact. They primarily generated financial reports filled with information but little insight and no recommendations for actions to drive better business outcomes.

This is not unique to Anders' former company but a general observation we have made working with clients worldwide. Finance professionals have been used to working with compliance and control responsibilities and not communicating their insights to business leaders. We often ask, when conducting training sessions, how important is communication for the career success of the participants? With slight variation, people respond between 9 and 10 on a 10-point scale. Our follow-up question is, how much formal communication training they have received during their career so far? Here, they respond between 4 and 5 on the same scale. This massive gap is hurting finance professionals' ability to communicate, not least to professionals outside of finance. If we do not fix this, companies will create less value. They will

Preface

not benefit from a data-driven approach and make suboptimal decisions.

In our experience, this is not because finance professionals do not want to improve their communication skills. Communicating financials to executives is one of the most popular training modules in our learning journeys with companies. Those who internalize the learnings transform their presentations and become more impactful. One transformation stands out in particular to us. This business controller's management report consisted of a giant Excel sheet with ten columns and 20 rows of data, including detailed explanations of the variances. After our training, he transformed it into two simple slides comparing actuals with the budget on four overall accounts and a summary slide with key insights and recommendations for the next steps. It would not be hard for management to understand this in minutes allowing the discussion to move to planning the next steps.

We know such a transformation would likely cause anxiety for many finance professionals as it is well beyond their comfort zone. No one can empathize with this more than us. In our journey towards becoming partners in a consulting company, we have often had to step outside our comfort zones. We are both introverts who have had to learn communication skills, build relationships and learn how to sell. This is

PREFACE

not easy; becoming an excellent financial communicator will be equally challenging.

It took Anders ten years to become a good business partner and communicator, and there are still many things he can learn and improve at. Many times in his career, he has stopped himself from doing what was right because it felt uncomfortable. Undoubtedly, this limited his career success and caused him to experience many frustrations. You are likely feeling some of the same frustrations, and rest assured that this book will help you overcome them and take your career to the next level. You should take comfort that many elements needed to become an excellent financial communicator come quite naturally to finance professionals.

You will likely not be particularly successful the first time you try any of the concepts we present in this book. However, those to whom you present will surely appreciate your efforts. Remember to ask them for feedback on improving your communication and presentation for next time. Every presentation you make will be better, and soon you will experience a world of difference in communicating financials to executives.

We frequently hear from individuals we work with that they get statements like 'Can finance really do that?' or 'This is the best financial presentation I have seen in years' when they transform their approach to

Preface

making management or business case presentations. We cannot guarantee that you will hear these exact statements, but we are confident that your audience will notice the improvement and appreciate your efforts.

Back on the ship in January 2017, both Anders and Christian experienced how, in a matter of few days, these finance professionals would learn to communicate differently and how they could present this elegantly on a business-relevant case they had only been introduced to at the beginning of the training. This proved that it was possible to do it differently; however, just like these finance professionals from the ship in Rotterdam, you must commit to changing your communication style over a more extended period. In our experience, it could take months, if not years, to master the principles of communicating financials to executives.

We believe in your ability to improve and know that the practical steps we will present in this book will quickly guide you towards a different way to present financials. You may find this different way uncomfortable, but we encourage you to love the idea for at least five minutes and try it out before casting it aside. In our experience, financial communication makes the difference in career success for most finance professionals. Unfortunately, most finance professionals struggle significantly today. We hope this book will be the famous line drawn in the sand where you say 'Enough!' to poor financial presentations and go down a different path. We are here to support you on the new path and wish you good luck reading the book and trying the new principles for communicating financials to executives.

CHAPTER ONE

WHY FINANCIAL COMMUNICATION TO EXECUTIVES REQUIRES SPECIAL ATTENTION

Everything we do as finance and accounting professionals eventually boils down to a moment of communication. Hit send on an e-mail. Stand in front of the leadership team. Be approached by a business leader at the coffee machine. Design a self-service dashboard. You can keep adding examples. These are all moments of communication.

In these moments of communication, we should harvest the fruit of our labor. All the long hours we use to analyze the numbers to understand what is happening and the underlying root causes. Now, we need to reap what we have sown. Unfortunately, we often fail to adequately articulate our ideas and insights. That is a real shame!

It hurts our careers and, even worse, our business results. Executives are screaming for us to deliver insights from the financials and beyond. They receive pressure from investors, the board, the CEO and stakeholders from the broader society. They need to make decisions much faster today than just a few decades ago, and the rate of change and volatility is only increasing.

It is easy to blame it on the executives. You have done the analysis and prepared the presentation. It is all there. You need to look at it and figure it out. However, that is only how it seems from our perspective. Most executives are not 'numbers people' and, indeed, not financial people. It is not intuitive for them to understand our analysis and numbers. They need us to communicate in a way that is simple and easy to understand and leads to tangible actions.

Our experience is that most finance and accounting professionals cannot do this. We will dive into the challenges they face in the next chapter. However, we typically communicate in too many details, with no apparent structure and with no obvious recommendation. This is very ineffective and leaves executives to make pure gut or experience-based decisions that are bound to be suboptimal.

THE PRESSURE IS MOUNTING ON EXECUTIVES

Executive tenure has been on a downward trend for decades, and there is widespread short-termism in the corporate landscape. In many parts of the world, executives only steer towards the next quarterly earnings release, and if the company is owned by private equity, the pressure is even higher. In this environment, executives need to deliver results, and they will grasp almost anything to help them make better decisions.

Most executives do not have a financial background, and even if they get some financial exposure on MBA courses or similar, that is not enough to give them solid financial acumen. In addition, they are very busy people with limited mental capacity. On any given day, they may have six to ten meetings where presentations are given, and people down the ranks are pushing for decisions to be made. That is why they need solid data to back their decision-making.

Data-driven decision-making has been a strong mantra amongst executives in the past decade. They understand the power of Big Data and use Data Science and Advanced Analytics to harness it. All they ask is that the insights derived from the analysis are communicated in a manner they can easily comprehend.

Understanding that a decision backed by data is not necessarily good is essential. On average, it is a better decision than one not backed by data. However, it needs to be paired with the experience of business leaders and a facilitated dialogue between them. This plays a vital role in removing bias from decision-making and ensuring that the assumptions made are documented and can be followed up on.

INSIGHT × INFLUENCE = IMPACT

The benefits of making data-driven decisions are undisputed, and you will be hard-pressed to find an executive who will refuse to listen to insights that can improve a specific decision. It is not enough to be right, as we must gain buy-in and acceptance for our insights to be factored into decision-making. We have put the relationship between insights and what we label 'Influence' on a formula. We express the ability to create an impact, e.g. increased value creation (Figure 1.1).

Figure 1.1 The Impact Equation.

An insight can be defined as a novel piece of information that enables executives to make a better decision. Thus, it is an unexpected shift in the way we understand things. In other words, insight is new information that challenges our existing understanding, causes us to re-examine our assumptions and potentially changes our perspective (Dykes, 2020).

Influence is perhaps more intangible to define. However, we can refer to the Buddha's words: 'An idea that is developed and put into action is more important than an idea that only exists as an idea'. Restated, this means influence moves your insight from an idea to something acted upon. How do finance professionals influence executives? We can break it down into three distinct parts.

1. **Be customer-centric:** Influencing business stakeholders by empathizing with them to propose relevant solutions that address their challenges – not just financial issues.

2. **Communicate with impact:** Influencing business stakeholders by being expert communicators who can leverage divergent and convergent thinking to explore win–win outcomes.
3. **Lead the way forward:** Influencing business stakeholders by making clear recommendations that pave the way forward while also daring to drive the implementation of your ideas.

Influence goes beyond communication, but it is a critical element. We could rephrase the three parts: why we communicate, what we communicate and how we communicate.

WHY: We communicate to address the critical priorities of executives. This also means there is no purpose to communicating if you are not working on a problem that interests the executive.

WHAT: We communicate insights derived from our financial analysis and problem-solving processes with a clear recommendation on addressing critical priorities. This also means that communicating has no purpose if you do not have relevant insights to address the priorities.

HOW: We communicate in a way that is easily understood by executives, making it straightforward to consider our insights into their decision-making process. This also means that if your communication is not tailored to the executives' needs and preferences, there is no point in communicating your insights since they are not likely to be considered.

This book focuses on the HOW and presents a simple framework for financial communication that builds on Barbara Minto's Pyramid Principle (Minto, 2010). We fully recognize the importance of WHY and WHAT, which we will now briefly review.

THE PURPOSE OF FINANCE

The finance function in companies has distinct purposes. One is compliance, which is governed by rules and regulations. Another is control, which is bound by promises made by executives, e.g. in the strategy or a budget. The final part is advisory, to drive value creation through improved decision-making, and it is not stipulated anywhere but through our ambition to create an impact.

- **Compliance:** All companies must abide by specific rules and regulations. Regarding financials, this could be accounting practices, e.g. IFRS or GAAP, filing responsibility for financial statements, etc. Executives likely do not care much for this part; however, compliance will keep them out of trouble, so they expect the CFO to handle these matters.

- **Control:** Most companies make financial commitments through budgets or similar documents. For listed companies, these expectations are communicated to the market, and failure to meet expectations may have significant financial consequences. Finance, therefore, must exercise control over the progress of meeting expectations. This includes internal financial reporting and ongoing follow-up with executives on how they are performing.
- **Advisory:** This element of data-driven decision-making is at the core of what we cover in our book. However, it is possible that executives already make great decisions and value above expectations is created. Hence, they may reduce Finance to an automated and outsourced service if they do not feel that Finance contributes positively to making better decisions.

To remain relevant, we must deliver on the advisory part. That reason alone should convince CFOs and senior finance leaders that investing in increasing their teams' ability to communicate financials is essential. However, investing in and significantly improving this ability is not enough. We must also prove that our efforts are making an impact. Here, we can highlight three specific measures.

1. **Business results:** Finance succeeds when the business exceeds expectations, as we are all in the same boat. This simple relationship can trickle down to all finance-to-business relationships in the organization. It should be reflected in the personal objectives of finance professionals who support executives in reaching their goals.
2. **Customer satisfaction:** Executives see value in having Finance at the table. As mentioned, it is entirely possible that executives can deliver great business results without advice from Finance. Hence, we must ask them if they think our advice contributes to reaching their goals.
3. **Value interventions:** Finance identifies and implements real business improvements. Finally, executives may be successful without our advice yet they are happy with the support they get. Perhaps they simply appreciate getting the monthly numbers on time and that we are on top of compliance and control. Therefore, we must be able to drive real business improvements and document the impact. Furthermore, we must be able to articulate precisely what we did that drove these improvements.

The WHY of financial communication should now be crystal clear. If we want to create an impact, we may even label it as a burning platform for Finance. If we do not make an impact, we may be reduced to an automated solution driven by artificial intelligence.

THE VALUE OF FINANCE

To earn a seat at the table, we must bring something unique that business leaders do not know. Earlier, we labeled these as insights, and we can further divide them into three distinct parts.

- **Running the business:** Insights that allow daily business operations to run efficiently to ensure consistent quality and continuous delivery of products and services.
- **Changing the business:** Insights to help drive business optimizations and process improvements to improve the business and run more effectively.
- **Growing the business:** Insights related to change initiatives, business cases and investments to explore opportunities related to new processes, products, or markets.

Insights are defined more broadly than just financial insight. Analyzing financials is often our starting point; however, when exploring root causes of variances between, for example, actual and budget, we quickly expand into business processes and even external events and trends. Hence, when we combine financial and non-financial data, we generate even more valuable insights.

Often, the executives we work with will better grasp non-financial data as it is closer to the specific actions they cascade into the organization for execution. Still, they are time-poor and will not do the analysis themselves, which leaves the door open for Finance to utilize our analytical capabilities to analyze data more broadly.

This is our opportunity to bring something unique to the table and, we might say, show the actual value of Finance in a company. We can be sure that executives will find someone who will if we do not do it: either hire analytical staff in their team or ask consultants to come and do the work. The decision to 'do it themselves' or ask Finance to do it boils down to our ability to communicate the insights, which brings us back to our starting point.

Finance can add significant value and create an impact. We do that by generating insights and influencing decision-making. All that stands in our way is our ability to communicate financials and insights to executives meaningfully.

THE INTRINSIC MOTIVATION FOR FINANCE PROFESSIONALS

We will soon address the specific challenges that finance professionals face when communicating financials to executives. However, it also makes sense to explore the intrinsic motivation of finance professionals to change what they do today. Before we explore the external factors, i.e. why executives need us to communicate financials better, it should also matter to us that we do things differently. We can guarantee that change will not happen if there is no desire to change.

We can take a starting point in the work that CFOs do. They communicate financials both externally and internally. The impact on their ability to communicate is clear. Try to join quarterly earnings calls with listed companies and observe the company's stock price. The words used by the CFO could either pull the stock price up or down. Not least, their ability to effectively answer questions from analysts is paramount in maintaining the company's credibility, credit rating and attractiveness in the stock market.

There have been many almost catastrophic examples of poor external communication. A great, more recent example is Lyft's communication of earnings expectations for 2024 when they published their 2023 Annual Report. They communicated that their profitability was expected to expand by 500 basis points. The actual expectation was 50 basis points. The stock price went on a rollercoaster ride that ended poorly (Stempel, 2024). What an embarrassment for the CFO!

CFOs also frequently make high-risk internal communications. They are in close contact with the board of directors and the executive management team. Most likely, the CFO does not prepare the presentations but remains the face of them and, therefore, must ensure that they satisfy the WHY and WHAT of financial communication as reviewed earlier. In every communication, the CFO's job is on the line. Communicate well and the CFO has a significant impact. If the CFO fails to communicate in a way that changes anything, the CFO is soon relegated to a compliance and control role.

We all go to work to do something meaningful and have an impact. That is true for CFOs and other finance professionals alike. Hence, being on top of both internal and external financial communication should be highly motivating.

COMMUNICATING FINANCIALS TO EXECUTIVES

THE JOB IS ON THE LINE

It may sound dramatic when we say the CFO's job is on the line in every communication. Probably, no one is let go for poor communication. However, CFOs log the shortest tenure of CXOs in the C-suite at the largest listed US companies, as an example (Noto 2022). We see this as a clear sign that CFOs are struggling to deliver the value that CEOs and the board expect of them.

The lack of impact is not limited to communication; other elements play into the equation when driving value creation. However, if all CFOs were expected to do was compliance and control then we would likely see very long CFO tenures. The burning platform is obvious: a more positive narrative exists for CFOs to change.

CFOs want to be involved in making their company successful. Compliance and control do not play a significant factor in that. Instead, CFOs should drive strategic value creation by forging a compelling vision and strategy for the company with the CEO. This involves making clear choices of where to play and how to win, which is connected to the terminology of the Playing to Win framework by A. G. Lafley and Roger Martin (Lafley and Martin, 2013).

More importantly, CFOs should design a management system that creates an effective cascade and feedback loop for the strategy. This work is laden with moments of financial communication and plays a critical role in realizing the strategy and creating the expected value. Beyond the core element of strategic value creation, CFOs are increasingly involved in topics beyond finance. This includes Environmental, Social and Governance (ESG) matters, cybersecurity, talent management and more. While these matters do not relate directly to financial communication, CFOs must translate the impact of these topics into financials to elevate their importance.

CFOs and finance professionals alike should find all this exciting. However, a license to play in areas beyond the core of finance is the ability to communicate financials. Otherwise, we only get to do the leg work and heavy lifting. Someone else will steal the glory, and we might find ourselves in the statistics of short-tenured finance professionals sooner rather than later.

ALL WE NEED IS A FRAMEWORK FOR FINANCIAL COMMUNICATION

It should be clear now why executives need us to improve our financial communication and why we would want to improve ourselves. However, it will not be easy, as we face many challenges, and we will highlight the three main ones in the next chapter. We need help to develop and transform our communication. That is our intention with this book!

We will provide a simple, practical framework for financial communication to executives that is easy to apply in your daily work. We will provide many practical examples and a small case study as a storyline throughout the book, showcasing the development we must go through. Providing the framework is only the first step. You will need to practice these ideas in your presentations, and you will not knock it out of the park on the first try.

We know from experience how challenging it is for finance professionals to transform their communication. We have seen it from training thousands of finance professionals during our careers. We see it daily in presentations we review for clients and individuals who come to us for advice on improving their reporting and executive presentations. We also hear many objections about why the current way is necessary and experience much resistance to change. All we ask you to do is to love the ideas we present in the book for five minutes. You will not know if it works until you try it, and we have yet to encounter finance professionals who said it did not work for them after applying it for a little while. Please do yourself a favor and try it out, too. Let us start by showing you how.

CHAPTER TWO

THE STRUGGLES OF FINANCE PROFESSIONALS TO COMMUNICATE FINANCIALS

We have now discussed why it is vital for executives that we communicate financials effectively to them. We have also reviewed what our motivation in doing so should be. This should create both an awareness and a desire for us to start communicating differently. Before we turn to how to communicate differently, we will review some of the main challenges we have encountered when finance professionals communicate financials. We will also introduce our case study, where we will meet Sarah, a Senior Financial Analyst at Solara Tech Inc., a mid-sized company specializing in developing and manufacturing solar energy systems and battery storage solutions.

Our purpose in reviewing the challenges is twofold. On the one hand, we want to show how we empathize with your situation. On the other hand, we hope that you will recognize some of these challenges in your daily work. If you do not and this is not your situation, that is okay; perhaps this book is not for you. Our experience shows, that 95% of all finance professionals could improve their financial communication.

This number is not based on scientific research, but we would offer two data points. One is from all the reporting from finance professionals we see in our work with clients and previous industry experiences. The other is from asking simple questions: What is the result of your management report? Is it data, information, insights or a recommendation? Only 20% say they make a recommendation to their stakeholders.

As we discussed in the first chapter, insights and recommendations do not automatically lead to improved decision-making. Without influence, you will still have no impact. Hence, even among the 20% that offer a recommendation, many will fail to make an impact because of poor financial communication. That is why we feel comfortable stating that 95% of finance professionals could improve their financial communication.

The Struggles of Finance Professionals

THE THREE MAIN CHALLENGES

Understanding the need for improvement is one thing, but knowing what to improve is the next step. We can obtain that knowledge by discussing some of the main challenges that finance professionals face. Again, these challenges stem from our experience and should not be seen as a finite list but simply as some that we observe in almost all financial presentations.

The more concrete result of these challenges is that the audience to whom we are trying to communicate our financials loses their attention. This happens much faster than we may think. Research shows that the average attention span for people looking at screens has decreased rapidly in the past twenty years (Mark, 2023). It has gone from two and a half minutes in 2004 to just 47 seconds in 2023. You have probably also heard the popularized statement that humans today have shorter attention spans than goldfish (McSpadden, 2015)!

There is no reason to believe these results should differ for executives. We should have every reason to believe that they are even shorter. That is due to the number of meetings they attend and their daily decision-making load. They cannot afford to waste their attention on something not made with their needs and preferences in mind. When they encounter presentations with one or more of the inbuilt challenges the presentation is not worth their time. Let us now outline the three challenges.

- **Too many details:** Financial presentations are usually plastered with tables and numbers. Even when they are mostly visuals, e.g. a waterfall chart, there are either multiple callouts or the smallest variances are included on the chart rather than consolidated into an 'Other' category.
- **No consistent structure:** Financial presentations often seem like a random set of numbers in chronological order. We probably meant well in our presentation, but what are we trying to communicate? That is often lost in translation, and executives must spend significant focused time trying to dig it out.
- **No apparent recommendation:** Only 20% make an actual recommendation in their presentation. That means 80% are sharing information that leaves the heavy lifting to the executives themselves. It is almost as if you bring them problems and want them to find the solutions. That makes for minimal impact on your side. Granted, you may share some valuable insights with no recommendation. In that case, you need to facilitate a process that leads to a decision.

We do not intentionally succumb to these challenges; we want to be as impactful as possible. There are many reasons why communicating financials often ends like this, and we will address some of them now.

SHARING TOO MANY DETAILS

Anders has a saying when he discusses executive communication with finance professionals and runs training, 'Know, but do not show, the details'. This is hard for finance professionals to accept. Here are some of the common objections we hear.

- 'I need to share all the facts in case the audience asks questions'.
- 'My stakeholder is very detail-oriented and always asks for the details'.
- 'I want to make sure all the numbers are in there just in case they want to go through them on their own time'.
- 'If I do not share all the facts and details, my audience might think that I am hiding something and trying to deceive them'.
- 'I know there is no getting around my CFO if there is not a complete set of financials in the monthly reporting'.

You probably have your objections, too, but are there any merits to these? The simple answer is 'No', but let us expand on this. Undoubtedly, we need to know the details of the financials and be able to answer most questions. We should even be able to anticipate most questions upfront and be well-prepared. Would that also put us in the best position to lead executives through the numbers?

That answer is obviously 'Yes', but it extends beyond this. It means we are also in the best position to separate what is essential from what is not. We need to help our stakeholders focus on what is essential, and if we are not sure, we can always check in with them before the monthly meeting. Here is an example of how that works.

Anders once supported a VP and a team of product managers, and there was a monthly meeting to review the individual products' profit and loss statements (P&Ls). Before Anders took over the role, these meetings consisted of a standard reporting package filled with numbers and tables, with only a few comments and insights. In addition, Finance was usually too busy to analyze the numbers properly; hence, an hour-long meeting often got cut short, or the product team started discussing other matters.

Eager to turn this around, Anders checked in with the product managers before his first P&L meeting to see what concerned them. They each highlighted some issues that would certainly not be covered by the standard slides. Anders, therefore, prepared an ad hoc analysis addressing their concerns. Instead of leading with the standard slides, Anders then led with the ad hoc analysis, leading to a good discussion and further issues to be explored. Despite only scratching the surface of the issues, the most senior product manager still said as they walked out of the meeting room, 'That was the best P&L review we have had in years!' All it required was to focus on their priorities and potential headaches rather than sharing detailed slides with tables and numbers.

All the details were still available in the appendix should they want to see them or have more detailed questions that the high-level storyline shared by Anders could not answer. However, they did not ask questions about the details, and in subsequent reviews, the details were never reviewed; instead, they evolved organically according to their changing priorities. Any finance professional could follow this approach and avoid having to give detailed financial presentations.

HAVING NO CONSISTENT STRUCTURE

Everyone loves a good story. That goes for executives, too. Stories usually follow specific structures that give us some predictability regarding what to

COMMUNICATING FINANCIALS TO EXECUTIVES

expect. We may not know the exact content of the story, but we know how we will be led through the story. This is rarely the case when finance professionals communicate with executives. Alternatively, there may be some structure, i.e. the first slide shows a table comparing actuals to budget. The next slide is a deep dive into revenue, followed by one on cost and finally on profits. The problem is that you likely lost your audience's attention before you get through these first few slides.

The issue here is that we treat all information equally. Even if we highlight the main variances, we still treat all variances equally. In real life, all information is not equal, and executives are looking for our ability to distinguish what is essential from what is not. This often goes wrong because the structure we think as finance professionals is helpful is different from the structure that executives think is helpful. As finance professionals, we value structures like these.

- **Financial statements:** We find it logical to go through performance using the structure of financial statements. That means starting from the P&L and ending with cash flow. Within each statement, we start with the highest-level account, e.g. revenue, and end with the lowest level, e.g. profit after tax. During our review of the financial statements we may cover some

The Struggles of Finance Professionals

of the main challenges we face; however, they are not ranked according to their importance and severity but on where in the financial statements they sit.

- **Completeness:** We value the completeness of information rather than its importance. For example, to explain the variance on an account, we find explanations that may cover up to 95% of the variance, so the last handful of explanations will explain only a few percentage points of the variance. This is a tedious exercise and makes for a very tedious presentation.
- **Starting with financials:** When we present the management report, we mostly start with the financials and explain variances. We usually only make financial comments. An example could be 'the variance to budget is 2.6 million USD, which is a 7% cost overrun caused by increasing variable costs'. We can all agree that this comment does not add much value, but this is often where we stop. Perhaps the slide, deep diving into variable costs, will explain more, but their attention is already lost.

Executives want something different from us. They want us to highlight the main issues the company is facing and make suggestions on how to solve them. There is a large gap between these two stories but there is a silver lining to this. All three structures we value as finance professionals have a very logical flow. That flow is needed to tell a good story to executives – not necessarily being a star reporter, a brilliant actor or even creating standout slides. All these things help; however, applying a logical and consistent structure to your storytelling matters the most. We will share how to do that in the following chapters.

MAKING NO APPARENT RECOMMENDATIONS

Any presentation we make should ideally lead to action. Otherwise, all we share is nice-to-know information that could just as well have been distributed via e-mail. We may not always know what the action should be, but if our presentations do not qualify and improve decision-making, we are wasting the busy executives' time.

Unfortunately, most finance professionals resist making recommendations. It is challenging to recommend actions to executives about their business, and it is safe to assume that they know best. We have observed some common barriers for finance professionals to lean out and make recommendations.

- **The 99%-mindset:** Many finance professionals suffer from 'The 99%-mindset'. That is, we will not make any statements about financials or business unless we are 99% certain we are correct and accurate. This seriously gets in our way for two reasons: (1) because it is almost impossible to be that certain about something that should lead to an outcome in the future and (2) because it takes a very long time to analyze the situation to that degree of certainty, meaning we will always be late with our recommendations.
- **They know best:** If you are a tax expert and are tasked with making a recommendation about the company's transfer pricing strategy, that is within your comfort zone. If you are a finance professional supporting the Chief Commercial Officer, you may hold back from making a recommendation about the company's pricing strategy. Shouldn't the CCO and their organization know best? This apprehension means that we attribute less value to our analysis and insights than the opinions of the CCO.
- **Summarizing:** Our analysis likely uncovered many facts about the current business situation during our analysis. An example could be that we have a variance in revenue, which our analysis shows is attributed to specific customers, products and markets. This information is

typically available in a company's business intelligence systems. However, rarely do we relate the different facts to each other or discuss them with sales leaders or reps to understand the underlying reasons. Hence, we resort to presenting the facts we have uncovered rather than leaning out and stating what it means for the company and what we should do about it.

We recognize that leaning out and putting forward our views is not easy, and you may feel like you need to put your job and career on the line. However, as described in the previous chapter, the job *is* on the line. If we do not do this, executives will find someone who will, and our role will be relegated to basic compliance and control. Therefore, rather than rejecting the notion that we need to make recommendations, we should learn about approaches to uncover insights and synthesize them into recommendations that executives can act on. This will be covered in the coming chapters.

MEET SARAH, A SENIOR FINANCIAL ANALYST

Sarah is a Senior Financial Analyst at Solara Tech Inc. who frequently presents financials to executives at her company. She made it to her current role by being very technically savvy in building financial models, orchestrating dashboards and doing in-depth analysis. Before her current role, she would usually hand off her analysis to her manager or a more senior analyst to prepare the presentation for management. That is why she never gave much thought to presenting financials to executives, until now.

In her first few presentations, Sarah prepared a standard management report comparing actuals to budget and the latest forecast. The presentation included commentary on the main deviations and highlighted key gaps for management attention. She would then dive into specific accounts, showing waterfall charts on the main movements and making callouts with explanations. She had given little thought to her audience except expecting them to follow the presentation and naturally ask questions.

Initially, there were some questions and a rather technical dialogue around deviations. However, the dialogue had recently died down, and the meeting would always finish early. Sarah also noticed that seemingly no actions were taken after the meeting, and the main gaps would persist from month to month. Could the leadership team have other priorities, or was she not doing these presentations right?

Sarah signed up for a course on executive communication to get some tangible and practical tips and tools to present in a better manner to the leadership team and catch their attention. The course was designed explicitly around financial communication. Sarah was excited about turning her hard work into insightful presentations leading to action and improved performance.

We will follow Sarah's journey throughout the rest of the book to learn about her progress and see how she could use the tools and concepts we will introduce. We will also show you her finished product when she prepares a perfect management presentation. We hope you will be inspired by Sarah's journey and treat this book as your own course on executive communication of financials. In the next chapter we will introduce the framework for financial communication and discuss how it applies to management reporting and presentations.

CHAPTER THREE

FIVE STEPS FOR COMMUNICATING FINANCIALS TO EXECUTIVES

We have covered why financial communication to executives requires attention and what challenges finance professionals currently face in doing it well. Now, we will introduce a five-step framework for communicating financials to executives. As mentioned, the framework builds on the Pyramid Principle by Barbara Minto. The overriding principle is that good communication is less about being an actor on stage, a journalist who can snoop up a story or creating brilliant slides. It is more about using a logical structure that catches the attention of the audience by focusing on issues that are important to them.

This is good news for finance professionals because we are good at that. For instance, our financial statements are built on logical structures, and if we boil it down, you could argue that everything we do in business ends up as a debit or a credit, logically balanced and in a complete presentation of financials. The challenge we have discussed is that this is not how to present the financials to non-financial executives. They will appreciate that everything balances, but they rely on us to be on top of that while they steer the business.

Instead, they need insights from us to make better decisions. It cannot just be any insight, though, as it needs to be insights that are relevant to the challenges they are currently working through. Otherwise, you will not catch their attention and quickly be shown the door. That is why being influential starts with a customer-centric approach and ends with a moment of communication. We briefly discussed the customer-centric approach in Chapter 2 and labeled it the WHY of financial communication. Before we share the five-step framework let us elaborate on what customer-centricity means for finance professionals.

Five Steps for Communicating Financials

TAKE A CUSTOMER-CENTRIC APPROACH

All finance professionals have customers. These are not your company's customers but the various stakeholders you work with internally. Some of these stakeholders also work in the finance function, and while those also have valid challenges to address, they are not the focus area of this book. Instead, we focus on business stakeholders not used to financial communication.

To serve their needs, you must first identify your main stakeholders, prioritize them and understand their current challenges. To address these, you can follow a simple three-step process. We call it the Customer Value Model.

1. **Identify your stakeholders:** This seems obvious to most, but we usually find many stakeholders we have not considered previously. It can be helpful to consider who your data suppliers are, e.g. accounting, and who are the receivers, e.g. business leaders. There could also be other relevant stakeholders, such as your peers, your manager, external stakeholders like auditors, etc. Most would have anywhere

between six and ten stakeholders, and usually business leaders are among them.

2. **Prioritize your stakeholders:** We could use many dimensions to prioritize our stakeholders but three works well for us. It is important to note that prioritization should initially be a relatively quick exercise and that combining all three dimensions determines your priority – not just importance.

   a. Importance: How important is the stakeholder in the general context of the company? Usually, this relates to job title and place in the hierarchy, but it could also relate to how well-connected they are across the company, etc.

   b. Strength of relation: The strength of your relationship with the stakeholder which we typically measure using the trust equation (Maister, Green and Galford, 2001).

   c. Customer satisfaction: How satisfied are they with the services they currently receive from you or Finance in general.

3. **Understand their needs:** Now that you have ranked your stakeholders, you should book a meeting with the highest priority stakeholders. The purpose of the meeting is to understand their current challenges, and you must start the meeting by stating that you are

Five Steps for Communicating Financials

there to help them succeed. Check your understanding of their needs before you end the meeting. Refrain from leaving with an implicit understanding but get their acceptance that you have understood them correctly and that it is clear which priorities you intend to help them with.

Anders once booked such a meeting with a new stakeholder he had got when he started in a new job. This was not the most important stakeholder, but Anders quickly realized that this stakeholder was particularly dissatisfied with the service he had received from Finance in the past. He clearly stated, 'I need Finance to do your job so we can do ours', as he felt he and his team were doing Finance's job. This was a clear sign that this stakeholder should receive a high priority from Anders since the dissatisfaction could easily damage other vital relationships and hamper Anders' ability to make an impact.

Using this three step process puts you in a position to work on challenges important to your stakeholders. This makes the analysis process much more efficient as you know which insights to generate. The overall goal is to move from data to insights in a structured and efficient manner while preparing to present the insights in a way that non-financial executives understand.

COMMUNICATING FINANCIALS TO EXECUTIVES

FROM DATA
TO INSIGHTS

We are not short of data in Finance, and we can easily spend all our time analyzing it. However, we need to move things along and ultimately generate insights. The first step will be to sort the data and arrange it in a useful way. This is typically done using various business intelligence tools or spreadsheet cubes that provide easy access to the data.

A pivot table in a spreadsheet is not a helpful way to present data. Instead, the data should be presented in more visually appealing charts or graphs to make it easily digestible. Most management reports coming out of Finance will look like that, and likely they will have some explainers for executives to understand what happened and why. However, this is not insightful as it usually tells something they already know. They may not know the exact number, e.g. +4.2%, but they know it is a range between +2 and +6%. Hence, the exact number does not aid their decision-making as it is not a new perspective.

Instead, we must go behind the numbers and find the story in the data. This is rarely a desktop exercise but involves talking to various stakeholders in the business and using problem-solving techniques to uncover root causes and potential solutions. The process starts by asking, 'So what?'. Let us say our revenue is up by 4.2%, a +1.3% variance to budget driven by an uptake in two key markets. So what? Is it good or bad compared to the market situation? Do we have the delivery capacity to do even more? Could we expect this positive variance to continue? Could we have observed a direct correlation between the sales pipeline and the revenue uptake?

We could ask many more 'So what?' questions, but you get the idea about the next steps in going from data to insights. The next, even more critical, step is going from insights to action, and this starts with asking the following question, 'Then what?'. We are continuing the above example with the positive revenue variance we figured out that there was a strong correlation between the sales pipeline and the uptake in revenue. However, we also learned that our delivery capacity is near its maximum, so continuing at this pace would carry some risk. At the same time, the sales pipeline looks promising, so we might miss a significant opportunity if we do not act now. The answer to 'Then what?' becomes 'We should look into ways to increase our delivery capacity'.

Imagine that you did not ask, 'So what?' but only shared the positive revenue variance with simple explanations. Everyone would probably leave the monthly meeting feeling good about the situation and continue business as usual. Next month, it will be a very different story. The strong sales pipeline would have pushed delivery capacity above its maximum, leading to delays, poor product quality and dissatisfied customers. What a disaster, given that executives could have acted to increase delivery capacity and harness further uptake in the market. Instead, you see your competitors run with the increased revenue and your financial performance suffering.

This is the power of two simple questions we rarely ask in Finance: 'So what?' and 'Then what?'. Remember that you are not expected to have all the answers but rather be the one asking the questions. You need to do some analysis to put yourself in a position to ask the right questions, of course, but it is not from the analysis itself that the answers will be derived. We may still fall short even if we ask the right questions since we still need to present our insights to executives for decision-making. We will introduce the five steps for communicating financials to executives.

FIVE STEPS FOR FINANCIAL COMMUNICATION TO EXECUTIVES

The simple principle behind the five steps is top-down communication. Start with the most important information first to drive decision-making and only, if needed, share facts and details to underline your insights or proposed actions. Too often, finance professionals communicate bottom-up, which is why they lose the attention of executives within just a few minutes. Instead, follow these five steps:

1. **Info:** What is the financial status?
2. **Insights:** What are the key attention points?
3. **Recommendation:** What can we do about it?
4. **Evidence:** How can we back it as a good idea?
5. **Action:** How do we get started?

In the following chapters, we will explore the five steps in depth. Below, we will provide a high-level introduction to each step, followed by a check-in with Sarah about her progress from her executive communication course.

INFO

This is how we open our presentation, and the objective should be to briefly outline the financial results, status for the period and overall drivers. If you have 30 minutes in a meeting to discuss the monthly performance, this section should take at most five minutes. Your starting point is the numbers; after all, that is the unique perspective we can

COMMUNICATING FINANCIALS TO EXECUTIVES

bring to the table as finance professionals. Present the financial results for the period and explain significant positive and negative deviations. Credibility should be your main trait when presenting the financial status. That means you must be prepared, factual and know the numbers. A key point here is not to show all the numbers but only key figures and deviations. When you show too many numbers you likely lose the audience's attention or risk receiving very detailed questions irrelevant to improving the overall performance. You should leave the detailed tables in the appendix, and if you have questions, you can always refer to those slides highlighting your deep knowledge of the numbers.

Here is a summary of the top tips for nailing this first section of your presentation:

1. Be factual.
2. Know but do not show the details.
3. Use visuals to communicate.
4. Avoid using too much finance jargon.

Following these top tips and forgetting the remaining four steps will significantly improve 95% of all financial presentations. Take this step seriously, even if it is not where most of the value is added.

INSIGHTS

Here we focus on a few critical issues worth bringing to management's attention. This is where we showcase our ability to separate what is important from what is not. We should investigate the story behind the numbers and uncover the challenges we face or opportunities that have presented themselves since we last reviewed our performance. A helpful approach is to check-in with the various executives before giving the presentation to ensure that the insights presented are relevant to the critical priorities on their minds at that specific time.

We should seek to enhance our understanding of their challenges or opportunities through analysis, quantification and qualification. As mentioned earlier, to develop insights we must discuss our analysis with various business stakeholders to get their take on the current situation. We can rarely derive relevant insights from pure analysis alone.

At the meeting, we spend around five minutes on this as a debrief on our findings rather than suggestions for discussion. If we have not included our audience or their team members during the analysis efforts, we may face many challenges from them. Checking in with them and speaking about their priorities means you often have a clear path to presenting your insights.

Here is a summary of the top tips for nailing this second section of your presentation:

1. Ask 'So what?' until you get to the core of the issue.
2. Synthesize your findings from your analysis and discussions.
3. Think like a journalist – what is the story?
4. Get buy-in to attention points before proceeding.

This is not easy, and few finance professionals do it well, so do not get frustrated if you do not nail it first time. Later we will describe the process of deriving insights in more detail and expand on these top tips.

RECOMMENDATION

Should you always include a recommendation in your presentation? Perhaps not. In many cases you will spend the next section of the meeting, for around ten minutes, discussing and brainstorming solutions to the situation you are facing. Still, showing initiative and proposing various actions to

Five Steps for Communicating Financials

address the issues is good. Essentially, your goal should be to propose an actionable solution that solves the challenges or takes advantage of the opportunities.

What is most important is that you show proactivity when taking charge of solving the issues. No one likes to have problems presented to them so that they can think about the solution. We would much prefer the solution presented, which we can qualify further or challenge if we do not think it makes sense. Sometimes, the solution is straightforward and we present one solution. Sometimes, we want to give people options without a clear-cut solution. Finally, we may be in a situation where we do not have a solution, and time is spent trying to find it together.

Ideally, we have already validated any solution with the main decision-maker before we present it at the meeting. We are not aiming to look smart in the meeting by presenting something the executives did not expect. No, we are trying to present an agreeable path forward to gain consensus during the meeting. This is also why we should not be concerned with offering recommendations. If, during our validation phase, we get negative feedback from the decision-maker, we know it is not the right recommendation to present anyway.

Here is a summary of the top tips for nailing this third section of your presentation:

1. Present options – no one likes to be told what to do.
2. Lean out – your opinion matters.
3. Prototype – make the solution visible to the audience.
4. Be assertive – positive and respectful.

Anders once had to give an important presentation to a steering committee on a project he had worked on with some colleagues. The steering committee was to provide a go or no go on the project, which was very important to Anders' career. However, the presentation turned out to be a non-event as he had checked in with all the steering committee members as part of preparing the presentation and recommendation. It was an excellent example of how to approach making a recommendation.

EVIDENCE

If all goes well, you never need to present this section, especially if the solution is straightforward and you are not presenting any options. When you get buy-in and acceptance of the recommendation, you are ready to move on. Suppose you are presenting options or face resistance when presenting the recommendation. In that case, you should prove why your recommendation is a good idea and will yield the desired results. You want to leave around five minutes of the meeting to convince your audience that yours is the right recommendation.

A simple approach to proving your recommendation is a good idea, so come up with the three most compelling reasons why your solution is a good recommendation. Each reason should be backed up by facts you uncovered during your analysis. Remember, arguments without facts are just opinions, and as finance professionals, we rarely get buy-in and acceptance by only presenting our views.

Facts can be more than just hard numbers. Statements from the executives, their team members and even external sources work well. They can also be past experiences from previous companies, anecdotes or trends. We want to win people over by convincing them our solution is the one that can solve their most pressing challenges.

Here is a summary of the top tips for nailing this fourth section of your presentation:

1. People never remember more than three bullet points.
2. Good evidence builds credibility for the solution.
3. Evidence can also be 'soft'.
4. Leave out facts that do not support your arguments.

Many finance professionals will feel compelled to present this section regardless of whether they have already received the buy-in and acceptance. That is because this is where we demonstrate our competence and the result of all the hard work we did on the analysis. However, showing off is not a goal of communicating financials to executives – getting to the right actions is.

ACTION

Congratulations! You got buy-in and acceptance of your recommendation, or facilitated a brainstorming session to arrive at the right solution. It is time to spend the remaining five minutes of the meeting presenting a plan to materialize the solution and getting buy-in for the next steps. Your audience is hooked on your solution, and wants to know how to implement it.

Making it easy for them to take the next step is essential. If the implementation plan is complicated, you will not likely get full acceptance; you may have to settle for the first step. If this is the case, break the plan down before presenting it, highlight the first step, and promise to come back and debrief with them the next time you meet to confirm you are on track and continue with the next steps of the solution.

Regardless, you should show them the plan, and show that you have considered various risks and opportunities and how to address them should

Five Steps for Communicating Financials

they materialize. Outline the specific details of the next steps and what they can expect to happen. This is especially important when they must take action to realize the recommendation. Finally, you should confirm what they are deciding on by asking for a 'Yes' at the end of the presentation.

Here is a summary of the top tips for nailing this fifth section of your presentation:

1. Summarize what was discussed.
2. Anticipate the most obvious questions.
3. Read their body language.
4. Remember to ask for a 'Yes'.

Too often, we leave meetings with a what appears to be a clear decision, yet with participants thinking that completely different things have been agreed upon. It is your responsibility to ensure that this does not happen. It would be a shame to throw all the hard work away at the finish line.

SARAH GETS TO KNOW HER CUSTOMERS

Sarah has completed the first day of her course on executive communication of financials. Now, she has some homework to do. Initially, she was

COMMUNICATING FINANCIALS TO EXECUTIVES

surprised that the first day did not include any content on executive communication. Instead, Sarah was introduced to the Customer Value Model and taught the importance of knowing your stakeholders and working on challenges that are important to them.

Sarah had now been tasked mapping her stakeholders and booking meetings with the management team members to understand their current priorities. Initially she thought the stakeholder mapping was straightforward as it would include the management team members. However, she quickly realized that more stakeholders were critical to her success in communicating impactful messages to the management team.

She had to consider not only the customers of her product but also the suppliers of the data, and those stakeholders she works with to enrich the data so they would become insights. In the past she had not given much thought to her suppliers but upon reflection she did have to spend a lot of time making manual corrections to the data she received and at least once every quarter the numbers would come late. This took time away from her to prepare the storyline for her presentation and was potentially the root cause for her sharing a standard presentation with few insights.

She also had to recognize that she had spent little time building relationships with the members of

Five Steps for Communicating Financials

the management team. Instead, she had reached out to them during the crunch time of the reporting period with a one-day deadline to comment on the numbers. This led to only shallow comments and perhaps even a negative sentiment towards Sarah, further diluting the value of the comments over time.

Now, she understood that before meeting with the management team members she would greatly benefit from speaking with the team members reporting to them. Not only would this help her prepare for the meetings, but it could also provide a fresh start in her relationships. Moreover, she accepted that she should also share what she learned from the management dialogues with her suppliers in the accounting team. This would elevate their understanding of what their output was used for and create a larger buy-in for delivering on time and of reasonable quality.

As she started having the meetings most stakeholders she spoke to were positively surprised about her initiative and were keen on restarting the relationship, seeing the benefits it would yield. Others were skeptical about this new approach and would take some more convincing which was utterly fair since this was a new way of working for Sarah and they had not seen this from any member of the finance organization before.

From her conversation with the management team members, she quickly learned that their minds

COMMUNICATING FINANCIALS TO EXECUTIVES

were in a completely different place than the standard financial slides she would show monthly. The Chief Commercial Officer struggled with an unproductive sales force and a weak logic between the sales pipeline and the business they would win. The Chief Operational Officer struggled with delivering products on time and precisely what Sales had sold. The Chief People Officer struggled with counting how many employees they had in the company but also mentioned many more value-adding challenges to solve.

This provided much clarity for Sarah regarding where to focus her efforts in the next monthly meeting. She was still keen to share the standard slides but she could put them in the appendix and dedicate most of the time to the challenges highlighted by the management team members. She was excited but slightly overwhelmed about how to start working on the various requests.

We will have to wait for the next chapter to see how Sarah gets along working on the management team members' most important priorities. This is also where we will deep dive into step 1 of the five steps for financial communication to executives.

CHAPTER FOUR

STEP 1: INFORMATION: WHAT IS THE FINANCIAL STATUS?

Having introduced the high-level, 5-step approach to communicating financials to executives, let us now dive into the mechanics of each step. Let us begin with step 1 – information, i.e. the current situation and financial status (Figure 4.1).

This part is your foundation and the starting point for your subsequent analysis and presentation of relevant insights. Think of it as the objective data representing the current financial situation from which you must uncover something meaningful to recommend to your stakeholders.

Despite it being the part on which you should spend the least time when presenting to executives,

Figure 4.1 5-Step Financial Communication Framework – Step 1.

the underlying data and information are the foundation on which you build your presentation. Thus, you often spend a significant amount of time extracting, cleaning and understanding the raw data during your preparation while only spending a little time on this part of the presentation itself. However, you can only construct a presentation that enables data-backed decision-making by truly understanding the data.

DEFINE AN OBJECTIVE AND TARGET STAKEHOLDER

To concisely present the current financial status, you must first define a clear purpose to guide your analytical process. Defining a clear purpose or objective before starting your data analysis is

Step 1: Information

paramount to ensuring the process is focused, efficient and yields actionable insights.

A well-defined objective guides the entire analytical process, from data collection to interpretation, and ensures that the analysis is relevant to your organization's and your stakeholders' specific agenda. To establish a robust objective, it is essential to address three critical questions: what entity is in focus? what timeline is in focus? and what decision is in focus?

What entity is in focus? Identifying the entity in focus is the first step in framing your analysis. The entity could be an organizational unit, a competitor, a customer segment or any other key element that is the focus of your analysis and following management presentation. For example, your analytical approach will likely differ if the focus is on an organizational unit, department or product line. Understanding which entity is under scrutiny helps select the appropriate data sources and metrics, ensuring that your analysis aligns with the business's specific aspects that need attention.

What timeline is in focus? The timeline defines the period over which the data will be analyzed, which is crucial for contextual relevance and comparability. Whether the analysis pertains to the last year, quarter, month or even a specific project duration, this temporal scope shapes the data selection process and analytical methods. For instance, examining a year-over-year performance might reveal long-term trends, whereas a quarterly analysis could highlight seasonal variations or recent changes. Clearly defining the timeline ensures that your analysis provides insights relevant to your target audience and their information needs.

What decision is in focus? Clarifying the decision the analysis aims to inform is perhaps the most crucial element of defining the objective. This could involve decisions related to resource allocation, investment opportunities, strategic planning or operational improvements. For example, if the goal is to aid resource allocation, the analysis might focus on identifying the most profitable products or departments that need additional funding. If the objective is to guide investment decisions, the analysis might evaluate the financial viability and risk associated with different projects or market opportunities. Clearly articulating the decision in focus ensures that your analysis is purpose-driven and provides actionable insights that directly support the decision-making process of your target audience.

Step 1: Information

It is a common mistake to refrain from properly scoping the analytical exercise before starting the data analysis and putting together a management presentation. Instead of defining a clear purpose, we open the spreadsheet and explore the data without establishing what should guide our efforts. Then we present the dataset to management with little or no interpretation.

Random data exploration might lead to interesting findings, but the likelihood of success increases significantly if a clear objective has been defined beforehand.

Consider Your Audience

An essential element in defining the objective entails knowing the recipients of your analytical findings. Often you know up front who the target audience of your final presentation is. This might be a specific stakeholder or management team that will use your findings to make informed decisions about crucial company matters. Examples include a management team reviewing a monthly report to adjust resource allocations or a leadership team deciding on a significant investment based on a business case.

Before you invest time and effort in financial analysis take the time to get to know your audience.

COMMUNICATING FINANCIALS TO EXECUTIVES

Place yourself in their shoes and consider what they care about and what they need to make the best possible decisions. It is essential to realize that the same things are not relevant to all audiences, as different stakeholders have varying priorities and information needs. For example, senior executives might prioritize high-level strategic insights that inform long-term planning and investment decisions. At the same time, department managers might focus on operational metrics and efficiency improvements relevant to their specific areas. Investors might be interested in profitability and growth prospects, whereas customers might care more about pricing trends and service quality. The CCO might be more interested in insights into the top line, e.g. revenue per customer or product, while the COO might be more interested in cost aspects of the P&L.

If possible, you should request a short briefing with your target audience where you get confirmation of your understanding of the needed information and what decisions are expected to be made based on your presentation. Strive for upfront confirmation rather than trying to guess the needs of your audience.

Tailoring your analysis to the audience ensures that the insights provided are relevant and actionable, avoiding the pitfall of overwhelming them with extraneous details that do not address their concerns.

Step 1: Information

Understanding your audience's perspective helps frame the analysis in a way that highlights the most pertinent data, thereby enhancing the effectiveness of your communication and facilitating more informed decision-making. Insights on analyzing your audience will be covered in detail later.

DATA EXTRACTION: ACCESS RELEVANT DATA SOURCES

Having set a clear objective for your analysis, the first step is to access relevant data sources that will allow you to present a realistic view of the current financial status. Most finance professionals can access data from multiple sources by leveraging various tools and technologies for data integration and analysis. Utilizing enterprise resource planning (ERP) systems, you can consolidate financial data with operational metrics, thus accessing a dataset with information from various parts of the organization.

Additionally, adopting business intelligence (BI) platforms enables integrating data from external sources, such as market trends, economic indicators, and competitive benchmarks, into your analysis. Knowing tools like Tableau, Power BI, or Qlik allows you to combine internal and external information to explore data in novel ways and present a nuanced view of the current situation.

By combining data from accounting software, CRM systems, supply chain management tools and external databases, you can better understand the entity of interest, enabling more informed and strategic decision-making. It is a common mistake for finance professionals to get stuck in the data immediately available in the ERP system without considering other data sources that might provide relevant nuances to the analysis. It is always relevant to consider if you can bring in other data sources – not just financials.

Regardless of how you access your data, it is critical to make sure that you know your data intimately – it is your prerequisite and license to play. You should always know the finer details despite not showing the data in your final presentation. Regarding data-backed presentations, you should think, 'Know, but do not show'. This means you must know the details if asked, but do not burden your audience with data overload as you present your findings.

Step 1: Information

DATA PREPARATION: BUILD ON A PROPER FOUNDATION

After establishing a baseline dataset for your analysis, cleaning the data and ensuring quality before commencing is essential. This ensures that you work with trustworthy data appropriately structured for subsequent analysis. You will lose all credibility if you present a financial summary based on flawed or incomplete data.

We all know that garbage in equals garbage out. Thus, if you do not ensure a proper data foundation, you cannot expect your analysis to yield anything useful for the target audience.

Master Data Management

A key element in ensuring a solid data foundation is proper master data management. Without going into details, master data management (MDM) involves the systematic administration of core business data, such as customer information, product details and financial records across various systems and processes. Effective MDM prevents data silos and discrepancies, thus providing a single, reliable source of truth that enhances the quality of financial analysis. With accurate master data, you can generate precise reports, conduct meaningful comparisons and confidently identify trends. Furthermore, good master data management is at the core of ensuring the existence of 'One set of numbers' – something that is considered a gold standard in any finance function today.

Financial analysis based on one set of numbers ensures consistency, accuracy and reliability in decision-making. When you rely on a unified data source it eliminates discrepancies and confusion from using multiple, potentially conflicting datasets. Ensuring a single set of numbers fosters a shared understanding of the company's financial health, streamlines communication across departments and reduces the risk of misinterpretation and disputes about data validity. Consequently, aim to work with a unified dataset recognizable to your audience since this will increase your credibility and make it easier for you to influence your audience's decisions.

Data Cleaning

Data cleaning is often needed before starting your analysis and presentation preparation, even with a unified set of numbers. Data cleaning involves

Step 1: Information

identifying and correcting your dataset's inaccuracies, inconsistencies and missing values to ensure its integrity and reliability. This process is essential because even minor errors can significantly skew analytical results and lead to misguided decisions. By thoroughly cleaning the data, you prepare it for analysis, making it easier to uncover accurate insights and trends. Moreover, clean data enhances the efficiency of the analysis process by eliminating the need to address data issues repeatedly. This preparation step ensures that your analysis is built on a solid foundation, leading to more precise and actionable outcomes.

Data cleaning can often be performed as part of getting data into a spreadsheet using queries. Queries allow you to extract specific data from large databases quickly and efficiently, ensuring that only the relevant information is imported into your spreadsheet. First, you must establish a connection between your spreadsheet software, such as Microsoft Excel or Google Sheets, and your data source, which could be a relational database, cloud storage or an enterprise resource planning (ERP) system. Using SQL (Structured Query Language) or other query languages, you can write commands to filter, sort and select the precise data needed for your analysis. Once the query is executed, the results are imported directly into your spreadsheet, formatted appropriately and are ready for further manipulation and analysis. This method saves time and reduces the risk of manual errors during data entry, ensuring that your dataset is accurate and comprehensive. Leveraging queries (often via Power Query in Excel) to populate spreadsheets allows finance professionals to maintain data integrity while enhancing the efficiency and effectiveness of their analytical tasks.

Chart of Accounts and Financial Statements

When it comes to financial analysis, a key element of data cleaning and preparation often entails structuring the data to facilitate the presentation of one of the most common financial statements, such as the balance sheet, income statement or cash flow statement. This involves organizing raw data into standardized formats and categories that align with the specific requirements of these statements. For instance, revenue, expenses, assets, liabilities and equity must be accurately classified and consistently labeled to ensure clarity and compliance with accounting standards.

A vital part of this process includes the ability to tie financial entries to their respective accounts in the Chart of Accounts (CoA). The CoA is a foundational element of any accounting system, providing a

Step 1: Information

structured framework for categorizing all financial transactions. Accurately linking each financial entry to its appropriate account ensures that data is systematically organized and easily traceable.

Linking your financial data to the CoA as part of the data preparation significantly eases the subsequent analysis. It enables both summation or drill-down into specific accounts to understand underlying trends and variances. This level of detail is often crucial for your stakeholders to make informed decisions. By prioritizing structured data preparation, you can efficiently produce precise and informative financial statements that support sound financial decision-making and strategic planning.

DATA ANALYSIS: EXTRACTING RELEVANT INSIGHTS

The analytical effort can commence by defining an analytical objective and establishing a proper data foundation. This is where your data is leveraged for financial modeling and analysis to extract relevant information, construct an overview of the financial status and identify potential insights.

The analysis will be guided by the objective defined previously, and there is no one-size-fits-all solution. However, horizontal and vertical analysis are two of the most common and foundational forms of financial analysis. Each offers unique insights by examining financial data from different perspectives. Let us explore each approach.

Horizontal Analysis

Horizontal or trend analysis involves comparing financial data over multiple periods. This approach aims to identify patterns, trends and growth rates by examining how specific financial statement items change over time. For example, horizontal analysis might involve comparing the revenue figures for several consecutive months, quarters or years to assess growth trends or identifying changes in operating expenses to understand cost behavior. The primary benefits of horizontal analysis include:

- **Trend identification:** By observing changes over time, you can identify positive or negative trends in key financial metrics, such as sales growth, profit margins or expense ratios. This information helps describe the current financial situation and often provides relevant hints about where the organization excels or can improve.

Step 1: Information

- **Performance evaluation:** Horizontal analysis also helps assess whether the company is improving, stagnating or declining in specific areas. By outlining the trend you can help management understand the financial situation of products, departments or the company.
- **Predictive insights:** Trends identified through horizontal analysis can also be used to prepare future projections and help in strategic planning. You can present potential future scenarios to management by extrapolating data from your horizontal analysis. This proactive approach can help senior leaders define relevant actions to influence future performance.

When performing horizontal analysis, financial figures for each period are typically expressed as a percentage change from a base period, providing a clear view of growth or decline. You might want to present your baseline as index 100 and the following periods as percentage changes from the baseline figure.

Despite its foundation in historical data, horizontal analysis is a powerful tool for forecasting future performance and identifying opportunities for improvement. By examining trends and patterns over multiple periods analysis can reveal consistent growth rates, cyclical fluctuations and emerging issues that might impact future outcomes. For instance, if a company consistently shows a 10% increase in sales each year, horizontal analysis can help predict future sales growth, allowing for more accurate budget forecasts and strategic planning. Additionally, identifying patterns of increasing expenses or declining margins can prompt proactive measures to control costs and enhance profitability.

By understanding past performance you can outline realistic goals, anticipate potential challenges and suggest ways to implement strategies to optimize future results. Thus, horizontal analysis should reflect the past and be essential to forward-looking financial management. However, beware of the pitfalls of extrapolation – you cannot always predict the future based on past trends. History is scattered with sudden disruptions that radically change the trajectories of products and entire businesses. Thus, horizontal extrapolation should be used carefully, and other data sources (market trends, competitor analysis, etc.) should always be considered.

Vertical Analysis

Unlike horizontal analysis, vertical analysis examines financial statement items as a percentage of a base figure within a single period. This method is also known as common-size analysis. For example, each line item is expressed as a percentage of total sales on an income statement. Each item is presented as a percentage of total assets, liabilities or equity on a balance sheet. The primary benefits of vertical analysis include:

- **Proportional insights:** This clearly explains each financial statement item and its contribution to the overall financial position or performance. By showing this to management you can provide important information about the cost structure of specific products or the importance of different products or service lines relative to each other. This can greatly aid decisions about resource allocation, etc.
- **Comparative analysis:** By standardizing financial data, vertical analysis facilitates comparisons between companies of different sizes or across different sectors, as it neutralizes the effects of scale. By performing vertical analysis across departments or competitors, you can outline the difference in operational performance and help management understand the key differentiators.
- **Efficiency assessment:** Vertical analysis can also highlight areas where expenses or revenues

COMMUNICATING FINANCIALS TO EXECUTIVES

are disproportionately high or low, aiding in identifying inefficiencies or strengths. By performing vertical analysis for various products or service lines you can inform management about what parts of the business add the most value to the collective profitability.

Vertical analysis simplifies financial data, making it easier to see relationships and proportions within a single period. Thus, it is handy for benchmarking and cross-sectional analysis.

As such, vertical analysis is a valuable tool for comparing products or departments within an organization by examining the relative size of each line item as a percentage of a base figure, such as total sales or total assets. By standardizing financial data in this way you allow for a clear comparison of the financial contributions and cost structures of different products or departments, regardless of their size. For example, in your company's income statement, vertical analysis can show the proportion of total sales attributed to each product line or department and the relative cost of goods sold, operating expenses and profit margins. This method highlights which products or departments are more efficient, profitable or resource-intensive, providing insights into areas of strength and opportunities for improvement. By facilitating these comparisons, you support strategic decision-making, helping managers allocate resources more effectively and optimize overall organizational performance.

Vertical analysis is also highly effective for comparing a company's performance to its competitors by standardizing financial data into common-size statements. This approach allows for meaningful comparisons across companies of different sizes within the same industry. For instance, you can use vertical analysis to compare your company's cost structure, profit margin and expense ratios with your competitors. This comparison can reveal relative efficiencies, cost advantages or areas where a company may be underperforming. By understanding how financial performance stacks up against industry peers, a company can identify best practices, benchmark its performance and develop strategies to improve competitive positioning. Vertical analysis thus provides valuable insights that can drive strategic initiatives and operational improvements, helping a company gain a competitive edge in the marketplace.

Variances and Deviations

A key element of almost any financial analysis is the identification of variances or deviations. This is crucial as it provides deep insights into the current financial status of an entity. Variance analysis involves comparing actual financial performance to budgeted or forecasted figures, highlighting differences that can signal underlying issues or opportunities. By examining these variances you can identify trends, inefficiencies or unexpected costs that need attention from management. A positive variance might indicate areas where the company outperforms expectations, suggesting strategies that could be replicated elsewhere. Negative variances, on the other hand, can reveal operational weaknesses, unanticipated expenses or revenue shortfalls, prompting corrective actions to mitigate risks.

Consequently, management is often more interested in seeing and discussing variances and deviations than the numerical value of items in your financial statements. Thus, you should be prepared to present relevant variances and deviations in your financial status overview – not just the face value of financial items.

Highlighting variances and deviations will help your stakeholders understand the organization's financial health, enabling more informed decision-making and strategic planning.

Using Technology to Your Advantage

Whatever analysis you decide to perform to present an overview of the current financial status you should aim to work smarter, not harder. This often entails taking advantage of modern technology to perform the required analysis. Modern technology has become indispensable for professionals seeking comprehensive analysis and identifying relevant insights in today's finance world. Advanced tools and software solutions streamline data management, enhance analytical capabilities and improve decision-making processes.

You likely have access to BI platforms. These tools offer powerful data visualization and reporting capabilities that allow you to create interactive dashboards, perform in-depth analysis and uncover trends and patterns that might be missed with traditional methods. Also, machine learning algorithms and predictive analytics further enhance the ability to forecast future performance, compare scenarios and identify opportunities for improvement.

Furthermore AI, particularly copilots and AI assistants, has revolutionized how finance professionals analyze and extract insights. These advanced tools leverage machine learning algorithms and natural language processing to automate complex tasks such as data aggregation, anomaly detection and trend analysis. AI copilots can assist you in real time by suggesting relevant data sources, highlighting significant patterns and even generating predictive models to forecast future performance. Also, AI assistants can quickly interpret large datasets, provide contextual recommendations and answer complex queries, enabling you to focus on providing strategic decision-making support rather than drowning in manual data processing. By enhancing financial analysis's speed, accuracy and depth, AI copilots and assistants can empower you to uncover and present actionable insights more efficiently and effectively.

By embracing these technological advancements, you can significantly improve your analytical capabilities and contribute more effectively to your organization's strategic objectives. Again, work smarter, not harder.

DATA SELECTION: PRESENT ONLY WHAT MATTERS

When your analytical work has been completed, only the most critical elements should be included in your final presentation. The baseline financial situation should be an ultra-condensed version of your analytical work. Including extensive data tables in the first pages of your management presentation is a common mistake, as this immediately creates an information overload. The detailed data

Step 1: Information

tables can often be excluded or moved to an appendix.

Instead present the current financial situation, e.g. the financial results for the period, by aggregating the numbers to the largest extent, which can be done without missing out on important information. If you can present a P&L with five lines instead of 20 lines without neglecting relevant information, you should aim to do so. After all, this part of your presentation should only outline the high-level status, as key points of interest, relevant insights and recommendations will be covered in the following sections. Only include what is relevant to achieve the purpose of your presentation, as defined during your preparation.

If possible, highlight substantial deviations by guiding your audience's attention with visual aids, e.g. red/green font colour or directional arrows. Be prepared to explain the likely underlying drivers of the deviations but keep detailed information and your key insights for the later section of the presentation. Let these three things guide you as you start preparing your presentation.

> **Nobody cares about your analytical process:** It is easy to be inclined to explain the analytical process that led to the results being presented. After all, you spent a long time gathering, cleaning and computing data. However, the process itself

COMMUNICATING FINANCIALS TO EXECUTIVES

is almost always irrelevant to management. What matters is the findings and their ability to aid relevant decision-making. Senior leaders do not care about how you calculate the variance but what that variance indicates in terms of the financial health of the company and the business decisions they must make. Consequently, you should avoid falling into the trap of showcasing your entire process and associated workload. It is unlikely to impress your audience and contradict the purpose of your presentation (unless your sole purpose is to show off your ability to handle multiple sheets in a spreadsheet workbook). Show the top of the iceberg, not everything under the surface.

Visuals communicate better than tables: The human brain processes images several times faster than it processes language (Dunn, 2023). Thus, data visualization is one of the most essential tools for preparing effective management presentations. If you want to limit cognitive barriers and make your message come across easily, strive to swap data tables for charts or other relevant data visualizations. A visual trend line is much easier to understand than numbers in a table. Refer to Chapter 9 for additional guidance on data visualization.

Step 1: Information

Avoid relying on finance lingo: You might be prone to using finance terms when presenting your findings to management – after all, this is the language spoken in the Finance department. However, you will likely face individuals from different departments across the organization when presenting. Thus, instead of talking about PE-ratios (price–earnings ratios), NPV (net present value) or contribution margins, you should aim to translate the information into a common language. This entails adjusting your wording to a non-finance audience by using non-finance jargon, making it easier for a broader audience to follow your train of thought.

MOVING FROM INFORMATION TO INSIGHTS

Having outlined the financial status based on the practices described above, finance professionals sometimes mistakenly believe that their job is done, thinking, 'I have presented the financial status; now it is up to others to make some relevant business decisions'. The job is far from done. Modern finance professionals are expected to present a retrospective view of financials and provide a perspective on potential root causes and recommendations for remediating actions to improve business performance. To do so we must review the financial status and ask, 'So what?' to define the most essential attention points and outline why they should matter to the audience. This is the next step of the 5-step approach to communicating financials to executives and the focus point of the next chapter.

SARAH'S DATA STRUGGLE

Full of energy, Sarah is ready to start delivering value to her stakeholders. She now has an overview of their priorities and an overall strategy for presenting her insights. However, she quickly runs into challenges as she starts her analysis. The data landscape at Solara Tech Inc. could be better, as the company has grown fast without building scalable solutions in the backend.

Sarah identified that Master Data Management is severely lacking and that the datasets she needs to analyze have many holes and empty fields. This means she must spend a lot of time cleaning the data in the first few months before it is usable for analysis. In the

Step 1: Information

past Sarah would have endured this cycle month after month, and it would have held her back in generating valuable insights. Now she identifies the root causes of each data issue and uses her newly established relationships with the leadership team members to solve them.

One example was found in her revenue analysis where there was an overall variance in the budget of US$ 5 million. She conducted a horizontal analysis to identify trends in revenue development over the past 24 months. Naturally, she wanted to explain the main changes, but as soon as she started to dig into the sales data she found revenue entries with missing customer and activity data. When she tried digging one step deeper into the sales activity data what she found needed to be revised, as most sales call entries included very little information about the customer and the purpose of the call.

None of this surprised her as it was evident from her conversations with her stakeholders that there were many data issues. Aligning with them on their priorities upfront made it much easier for her to address the problems. She would sit with a few of the salespeople and talk through the issues to understand what barriers they were facing. It turned out that they had to enter the same information multiple times during the lead-to-agreement journey, which was very annoying and led to too many errors in the data entry.

COMMUNICATING FINANCIALS TO EXECUTIVES

Because of these barriers, many of them had given up, not least because they did not get any benefit from it.

Fortunately, it was possible to change their current Customer Relationship Management (CRM) system and sales processes to tackle the barriers salespeople were facing. Having leveraged technology to make life easier for the salespeople, they were also happy to share their insights into the revenue developments that Sarah had observed. All that was left for Sarah to do was select the insights that explained most of the variance in revenue. She gathered enough intel to present the financial status confidently at the next monthly management meeting. She still needed to dig deeper into the issues, though, as she could only explain what the deviations in revenue related to and why they were occurring. She needed to uncover the root causes to suggest potential solutions. We will return to Sarah's story at the end of the next chapter.

CHAPTER FIVE

STEP 2: INSIGHTS: WHAT ARE THE KEY ATTENTION POINTS?

Having outlined the current financial situation in step 1, it is time to ask, 'So what?' to identify relevant insights for the audience (Figure 5.1). Asking 'So what?' means exploring why the target audience should care about what is being presented, i.e. the key attention points to be highlighted. Where the information about the current financial status presented in step 1 answers the question, 'What', the insights presented in step 2 are supposed to answer the question, 'So what?'

Figure 5.1 5-step financial communication framework – step 2.

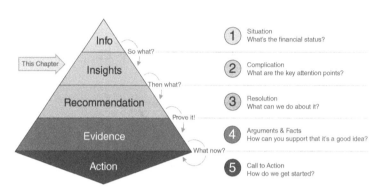

WHAT IS AN INSIGHT?

As described in Chapter 2, where the impact equation (impact = insights × influence) was introduced, insight was defined as a novel piece of information that enables executives to make better decisions. In other words, insight leads to an unexpected shift in the way we understand things, and as such insight is new information that challenges our existing understanding, causes us to re-examine our assumptions and potentially changes our perspective (Dykes, 2020).

Consequently, an insight is not just any piece of new information. The new information must be relevant to the audience's decision-making process. They must use the information to improve their

Step 2: Insights

decision-making and make better, more informed decisions than they would have made without the insight. An observation makes the audience go 'Hmm…' while an insight makes the audience go 'Aha!'

| Observation | 'Hmm…' | The cost variance month-on-month is +20% above expected |
| Insight | 'Aha!' | We have endured a once-off IT cost due to a security breach |

Stated differently, an insight is a finding that is newsworthy and noteworthy for the target audience.

Newsworthy means that the information is interesting enough to be reported. This implies that the information must be somewhat out of the ordinary and provide a perspective on something relevant to the audience. Furthermore, timely newsworthy information represents the most recent data or developments. The audience may not know it yet, making it fresh and compelling. A significant variation in financial numbers will often be newsworthy.

Noteworthy means that the information is worth taking a more profound interest in. This implies that the information is notable or remarkable and could have meaningful consequences for the business or the audience's specific area of focus. Noteworthy information addresses a question relevant to the audience or a problem they are trying to solve. It provides a deeper context or understanding beyond surface-level data by connecting different pieces of information to reveal a more significant trend, risk or opportunity. As such, noteworthy information often carries a sense of urgency, implying that the audience may need to act on this information soon to avoid risks or capitalize on opportunities.

In management reporting, there is often a noticeable gap between newsworthy and noteworthy. The information in management reports is often somewhat newsworthy, reflecting the latest developments in financials and business operations. However, finance professionals often fail to make the information noteworthy to the audience. Financial results and budget vs. actual deviations might be highlighted, but the 'so what?' question is missing. We fail to move on from step 1, the financial status, neglect creating a personal relevance to the audience and miss out on the opportunity to influence decision-making.

Suppose you are presenting the quarterly results to a management team, and have identified that your company's cash inflow has decreased by 15% compared to the previous quarter. This information is newsworthy as it reflects the most recent quarter's performance and is a novel piece of information that the management team may not yet know. It is a relevant part of the financial status. However, the information is not necessarily noteworthy. However, suppose you identify that the negative cash flow

Step 2: Insights

trend is caused by an issue with the automatic invoicing system that has led to an increase in unpaid invoices and higher accounts receivable (AR). In that case, the information becomes noteworthy to your CFO (and likely the CIO and others). The additional information about the cause-and-effect indicates an urgency and the need to take immediate action to realign operations towards corporate targets. It could impact the company's ability to fund strategic initiatives, pay down debt or distribute dividends if not managed. Since the finding indicates a source of the problem – accounts receivables – it is actionable as it guides management towards relevant mitigating actions.

To test whether you are presenting insights – information that is both newsworthy and noteworthy – you should ask yourself the following questions.

1. **Do they care?**

   Consider your intended audience and reflect on their concerns and interests. From their perspective, are they likely to care about what is being presented? The Chief Financial Officer, Chief Information Officer, or Chief Human Resource Officer (CHRO) do not necessarily care about the same things as they reside in different parts of the organization and hold very different responsibilities.

2. Can they act?

Consider if your target audience can influence the situation related to what is being presented. If they have no way of doing anything about the situation, or if the decision to act is outside their area of responsibility, the information might not be relevant to the audience. They might find it newsworthy, but it is not noteworthy if they cannot influence the situation. In this case, you are likely presenting to the wrong people (barking up the wrong tree), or you should focus on something more suited to the audience in front of you.

3. Does it impact?

Even if what is being presented is something that the audience might care about and could do something about, it is not the best use of management's time if the potential impact is limited. Impact does not necessarily have to be financial. However, if the information presented is unlikely to result in a significant outcome, there are likely to be other, more meaningful insights to be conveyed. You should always focus on what creates the most bang for the buck when presenting to executives.

Step 2: Insights

CATER TO YOUR AUDIENCE

What constitutes an insight depends on the target audience. As such, insights are contextual, meaning that they depend on what is essential to the receiver. A rapid shift in consumer demand is noteworthy and newsworthy to a Chief Commercial Officer but might not be particularly relevant to the Chief Information Officer.

The importance of knowing your target audience was introduced in step 1 when discussing defining the objective of your analysis and presentation. Understanding your audience's perspectives helps frame the analysis in a way that highlights the most pertinent data, thereby enhancing the effectiveness of your communication and facilitating more informed decision-making. This goes for the selection of relevant insights as well.

Consider why the selected insights are relevant to the audience, how they can use the information and where the information ties into their pre-existing understanding of the matters at hand. This means empathizing with your audience, putting yourself in their place and relating to their agenda, including potential opportunities and challenges. Only by being empathic can you identify what is important to the audience and what they might need to make better and faster decisions.

EMPATHY: PRESENT INSIGHTS RELEVANT TO YOUR STAKEHOLDERS

To reflect on your audience's motivations and the associated need for insights, try answering the questions below in order, from 1 to 7. This will allow you to 'walk in their shoes', understand their viewpoint and select relevant insights to highlight in your presentation.

1. **WHO is the audience?**

   Who are the individuals you are presenting to? What is their current situation, and what role do they play? You should have identified this at the beginning of your analytical process in step 1. However, it becomes even more critical now that you select the most important things to highlight in your presentation. You can only really hope to answer the 'so what?' related to the outline of the current financial status if you know who you are talking to and in what context.

2. **What must they DO?**

Ask yourself what the audience needs to do differently, i.e. what decision(s) they must make based on your presentation. Whether they are supposed to make an investment decision, reallocate existing resources, initiate a project or something completely different can guide you on what insights are important to highlight in your presentation.

You should also consider how the audience measures the success of what they must do. If you present a business case to management they may measure the success of the investment based on the expected net present value (NPV) or other form of return on investment (ROI). If that is the case you might consider including information about these values and the assumptions with which they are calculated.

3. **What do they SEE?**

Consider what your audience sees in the organization. What are they experiencing that might cause them to be concerned or optimistic? By considering what your audience experiences others doing you can address relevant concerns in your presentation. If management is experiencing multiple simultaneous resignations they

COMMUNICATING FINANCIALS TO EXECUTIVES

may be concerned about the employees' corporate culture, work–life balance or general workload. By recognizing this, you can add relevant insights about employee retention to your presentation.

4. **What do they SAY?**
Think about what you have heard your audience say about the matters. Consider if they expressed concern or excitement about specific organizational topics or challenges. By reviewing what your audience has expressed about the matter, you can potentially identify areas or topics that are more important to focus on than others. Even without pre-existing knowledge you can try to imagine what the audience is likely to say about what you are presenting or proposing. It is always relevant to consider the response you expect from what you are about to present.

5. **What do they DO?**
Reflect on what they currently do and what behavior you have observed. Current behavior often indicates the audience's priorities and what they see as urgent and potentially important. Imagine that you are aware that individuals in your audience are overseeing the transition of processes from one IT solution to another. You have seen them work on realizing efficiency

Step 2: Insights

gains as part of this effort. Based on this information, you may decide to include information about how the financials you are presenting have been or will potentially be affected by the new IT solution and associated efficiency gains.

6. **What do they HEAR?**

Consider what your audience may have heard before your presentation. They might have talked to business partners, employees or other trusted relations. Depending on how others might have expressed their opinion, your audience could have a predisposition to see what will be presented in a particular light. Suppose a Chief Operations Officer has expressed concern about production capacity or supply chain challenges. In that case, the CFO might expect to see a negative impact on the monthly or quarterly P&L. If so, you can adjust your presentation to address that topic.

7. **What do they THINK and FEEL?**

Despite our desire for rational thinking, human beings are rarely as rational as we would like to think. Good decision-making often arises from a balanced approach to data analysis and intuition (Farrell, 2023). The human brain is lazy, and we tend to make most decisions in what Daniel Kahneman coined as system 1 thinking. System 1 thinking is the limbic system, which makes fast and intuitive decisions guided by emotions (Kahneman, 2011). We'll return to the two systems of thinking in a later chapter.

Consequently, it is relevant to consider what your audience might feel or think about what is being presented. Try to identify their potential fears, frustrations and anxieties, as well as their wants, needs, hopes and dreams. By gauging your audience's emotional state, you can tailor your presentation to leverage their state to achieve your desired outcome. When the audience might have a negative view of your presentation's content, creating the right energy and engagement related to your proposal is imperative. If you can create excitement about the prospect of a specific outcome, you are much more likely to convince your audience to act on your information.

Verify Your Understanding

Considering the questions above to understand your stakeholders' perspectives will allow you to identify the most relevant attention points. However, even if you take the time to put yourself in your audience's shoes, you will never be able to read their minds. Consequently, getting buy-in to your selected attention points and recommendations before proceeding is always preferable. The most significant part of influencing a decision is often done before the official presentation.

If possible, communicate what you expect to present to key stakeholders upfront and ensure you understand the different views and perspectives on the matter. Get your stakeholders' point of view and acceptance that they also see the situation and key attention points as you do. Doing so will increase the chances of a successful management presentation as you avoid negative surprises and limit potential resistance from the audience.

Acknowledge Personality Types

In addition to reflecting on your audience's priorities, it can be highly effective to understand and acknowledge your stakeholders' personality profiles before selecting what and how to present. Different individuals process information and make decisions in different ways; some may prefer detailed data and analysis, while others might prefer high-level summaries and strategic implications. Some individuals have a process focus, others a people focus.

Many organizations leverage frameworks to articulate and discuss personality types to foster greater understanding and collaboration. Whether it is MBTI

(Meyers–Briggs), Everything DiSC, WholeBrain, SDI or another framework, the main idea is to categorize individuals based on their score across selected personality trait dimensions.

The Big Five personality traits (Kang, Guzman and Malvaso, 2023) referred to as the OCEAN model, encompassing Openness, Conscientiousness, Extraversion, Agreeableness and Neuroticism, serve as the foundational elements for most modern personality type frameworks. These five broad dimensions capture the essential aspects of human personality, each representing a range of behaviors, attitudes, and emotional patterns (Figure 5.2).

Whatever framework you use, you must tailor your presentation of insights to the audience's preferences. You might have heard that you should treat others like you want to be treated. In this case that is not true – you should treat others like they want to be treated. By tailoring your presentation to align with these preferences, whether addressing analytical thinkers who value precision or big-picture leaders who focus on vision and outcomes, you enhance engagement and facilitate better decision-making. This personalized approach makes your presentation more impactful and demonstrates empathy and respect for your audience's needs, ultimately fostering more assertive communication and better collaboration.

Step 2: Insights

Figure 5.2   The OCEAN model.

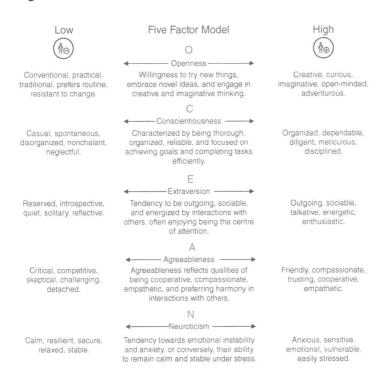

TYPES OF ANALYTICS

Having explored and identified your audience's objectives, you should have understood the key challenges or opportunities that would be relevant to bring to their attention. However, moving from step 1, the financial status, to step 2, the key attention points, and onward to step 3 – the recommendation – requires different tools from the analytical toolbox.

Each step warrants a different analytical approach – what is traditionally referred to as different modes or types of analytics. Step 1 requires descriptive analytics, step 2 warrants diagnostic and predictive analytics, while step 3 often involves prescriptive analytics. To guide you, consider how each mode of analytics links to the communications framework.

Step 1: Information →	Descriptive analytics
Step 2: Insights →	Diagnostic and predictive analytics
Step 3: Recommendation →	Prescriptive analytics

The different types of analytics (Figure 5.3) allow us to form a holistic view of a situation, thereby enabling data-backed decision-making that leads to actions that drive the business forward.

Descriptive analytics summarizes and interprets historical data to understand past events or trends. Descriptive analytics focuses on answering the

Figure 5.3 The four modes of analytics.

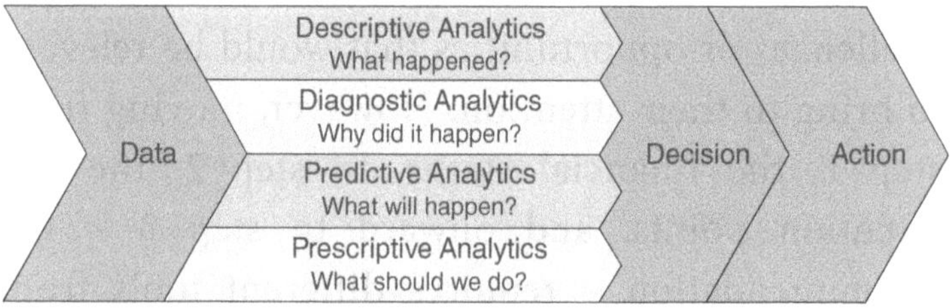

Step 2: Insights

question: 'What happened?' Examples of descriptive analysis used by finance professionals include:

- **Financial statement analysis:** This process summarizes historical financial performance through income, balance sheet and cash flow statements. Key metrics like revenue growth, profit margins and liquidity ratios are analyzed to provide insights into past financial health.
- **Trend analysis:** Tracks and visualizes historical trends in key financial metrics, such as sales, expenses and profits, to understand patterns over time.
- **Variance analysis:** Compares actual financial results to budgets or forecasts to understand deviations and their impact on performance.
- **Ratio analysis:** This analysis uses financial ratios (e.g. current ratio, debt-to-equity ratio, return on equity) to summarize a company's financial position and performance.

Diagnostic analytics concerns understanding and describing the root causes behind certain events or trends. Diagnostic analytics focuses on answering the question: 'Why did it happen?' Examples of diagnostic analysis used by finance professionals include:

- **Root cause analysis:** This investigates the underlying causes of financial outcomes, such as why revenue declined or why costs increased. It might involve analyzing cost drivers, customer behavior or market conditions.

- **Correlation analysis:** Examines the relationships between different financial variables (e.g. the correlation between marketing spend and sales revenue) to identify factors that may have contributed to observed outcomes.
- **Variance decomposition:** This process breaks down variances in financial performance to identify specific components (e.g. volume, price and mix) that contributed to the overall variance.
- **Drill-down analysis:** This type of analysis delves into detailed data (e.g. by region, product line or department) to understand the factors driving overall performance.

Predictive analytics is concerned with forecasting and estimating trends to predict what will happen in the future. Predictive analytics focuses on answering the question: 'What will happen?' Examples of predictive analysis used by finance professionals include:

- **Forecasting models:** Uses historical data and statistical techniques to project future financial performance, including revenue forecasts, expense forecasts and cash flow projections.

Step 2: Insights

- **Regression analysis:** Models relationships between variables to predict future financial outcomes, such as how changes in economic indicators might affect sales.
- **Time Series analysis:** Applies techniques to forecast future financial metrics based on historical patterns and seasonality.
- **Scenario analysis:** Evaluates the potential impact of different future scenarios (e.g. economic downturns, changes in regulation) on financial performance, allowing for the assessment of best-case, worst-case and most likely outcomes.

Prescriptive analytics is concerned with suggesting and recommending actions to influence potential future outcomes. The focus of prescriptive analytics is to answer the question: 'What should we do?' Examples of prescriptive analysis used by finance professionals include:

- **Decision trees:** Analyze different decision paths and their potential outcomes to recommend the best strategy, such as investing in a new project or entering a new market.
- **Monte Carlo simulation:** Uses probability distributions to simulate various possible outcomes and assess the risks and benefits of different decisions, such as investment or financing strategies.

COMMUNICATING FINANCIALS TO EXECUTIVES

- **Cost–benefit analysis:** Compares the expected costs and benefits of different actions to recommend the most financially viable option.
- **Real option analysis:** This extends traditional financial analysis by incorporating the flexibility to adapt decisions based on how future events unfold, much like financial options provide the right, but not the obligation, to make certain moves (e.g. buying or selling an asset) in the future.

In the communication framework, descriptive analytics is used for the 'what' in step 1, diagnostic and predictive analytics are used to outline the 'so what' in step 2 and predictive analytics aims to answer the 'then what' in step 3. Start by understanding historical performance with descriptive analytics, then identify challenges with diagnostic analytics, make predictions of future trends with predictive analytics and prescribe specific actions with prescriptive analytics. By integrating these different types of analytics, you can create a comprehensive, data-driven decision-making framework.

Unfortunately, much traditional financial reporting has focused solely on descriptive analytics, merely presenting historical figures and the financial results of past events without further analysis. This kind of historical reporting is not irrelevant, but insights that drive future business outcomes are rarely uncovered by merely applying descriptive analytics.

Diagnostic analytics dig into the causality of the data, identifying root causes and hidden connections. Predictive and prescriptive analytics focus on foreseeing potential future outcomes and identifying solutions and recommendations; this is needed in step 3 of our communicative framework, which focuses on presenting relevant resolutions.

TIPS ON HOW TO COMMUNICATE YOUR INSIGHTS

Whatever you select as the most relevant insights to present, you aim to convey your message to the audience without confusion or distortion. Even the brightest leadership audience still comprises humans with a limited attention span and mental capacity. Consider the following tips for presenting your insights to overcome communication barriers.

Tip 1: Golden Rule of Three

In the world of financial communication, clarity is paramount. Whether you are presenting to the board, potential investors or internal stakeholders, your goal is to convey complex financial information in an understandable and compelling manner. One of the most effective strategies for achieving this is carefully curating your content, adhering to the 'Golden Rule of Three'. The 'Golden Rule of Three' is a principle rooted in cognitive psychology, suggesting that people are more likely to remember and process information when presented in groups of three. Here is why:

- **Cognitive ease:** Research shows that the human brain naturally gravitates towards patterns and groups of three. Three points are sufficient to create a pattern, but not so many that the audience becomes overwhelmed or confused.
- **Memorability:** People are more likely to remember information that is presented in a structured and concise manner. Three points balance comprehensiveness and simplicity, making your audience more likely to retain the information after the presentation.
- **Focus:** Limiting yourself to three main highlights forces you to prioritize the most critical information. This discipline ensures that your presentation focuses on what matters rather than getting lost in the details.

Step 2: Insights

This rule is powerful in financial communication, where the subject matter can be dense and complex. When crafting your management presentation, aim to highlight three main points, i.e. key insights. These could be the most critical financial metrics, the most significant strategic initiatives or the organization's three most important risks and opportunities. By focusing on three key highlights you create a narrative structure that is more straightforward for your audience to follow and remember. In financial communication less is often more. By adhering to the Golden Rule of Three, you can create management presentations that are clear, focused and impactful. In a world where attention spans are short and information overload is a constant challenge, the power of three is a simple yet powerful tool for making your message stick.

Tip 2: Curate Based on Criteria

The selection of what to include in a management presentation must be a deliberate process, guided by specific criteria that ensure the most critical information is highlighted. Curating content based on criteria such as importance, urgency or impact,

COMMUNICATING FINANCIALS TO EXECUTIVES

can create an insightful and actionable presentation. Here are three key criteria to consider when curating content for a management presentation.

Importance: When curating content, the first criterion to consider is the importance of the information to the organization's strategic goals. Important content is that which directly supports the company's mission, vision or long-term objectives. To evaluate the importance, ask the following questions:

- **Strategic alignment:** Does this information align with the organization's strategic priorities?
- **Decision-making:** Is this information essential for making informed decisions to drive the company forward?
- **Long-term impact:** Will this information have a lasting effect on the organization's success?

Only content that meets these criteria should be included, ensuring that your presentation addresses the most critical aspects of the business.

Urgency: Next, consider the urgency of the information. Urgent content requires immediate attention or action to prevent negative consequences or to be able to capitalize on emerging opportunities. This criterion is crucial in a dynamic business environment where delays can lead to missed opportunities or exacerbated risks. To evaluate urgency consider:

Step 2: Insights

- **Time sensitivity:** Is this information related to a time-sensitive issue that requires prompt decision-making?
- **Short-term impact:** Will delaying action on this information negatively affect the organization?
- **Regulatory or compliance deadlines:** Does this information relate to upcoming deadlines or regulatory requirements that must be met?

Be cautious about confusing false urgency with what is truly urgent and important. We tend to perceive our priorities as important and urgent, even if these are comparatively less so compared to other organizational initiatives. We get stuck on what is within our sphere of interest while failing to remember that what seems urgent might seem utterly irrelevant to others. By objectively prioritizing urgent issues your presentation will prompt timely action, helping the organization stay ahead of challenges and seize opportunities.

Impact: The impact of the information is another critical criterion. High-impact insights are those that have the potential to significantly affect the organization's performance, whether positively or negatively. Impactful information can influence financial results, operational efficiency or market position. To assess impact, ask yourself:

COMMUNICATING FINANCIALS TO EXECUTIVES

- **Financial impact:** Will this information affect key financial metrics, such as revenue, profit margins or cash flow?
- **Operational efficiency:** Does this information potentially improve or hinder operational performance?
- **Market position:** Will this information influence the company's competitive position or market share?

Content that scores high on impact should be highlighted in your presentation, as it represents areas where the organization can achieve significant gains or avoid substantial losses. Criteria other than those presented above can also be used to curate what to include in your presentation. Criteria like relevance, risk or organizational change might also work if the circumstances demand it. It is up to you to select the most relevant criteria for your presentation.

Tip 3: Do not Just Summarize – Synthesize

In financial communication, the distinction between summarizing and synthesizing is critical. While both involve condensing information, the depth of analysis and the value provided to the audience differ significantly. Finance professionals

Step 2: Insights

must go beyond mere summarization to synthesize their insights, offering a cohesive narrative that guides decision-makers. This approach is akin to thinking like a journalist – focusing on the facts and the story that ties them together. Here is how summarization and synthesizing are different in management reporting.

Summarization: At its core, summarization involves distilling large amounts of data or information into a concise format. It is about capturing the key points or facts from a detailed analysis or report. For example, summarizing a financial report might involve listing the company's quarterly revenue, profit margins and main expenses. While this provides a snapshot of the data, it often lacks context or interpretation.

Synthesizing: Synthesis, on the other hand, goes a step further. It condenses information and integrates it into a broader context, drawing connections between data points and providing an overarching narrative. Synthesizing financial data means interpreting the numbers for the business and identifying trends, implications and potential actions. It is about weaving the data into a coherent story that addresses the 'so what?' – why the information matters and how it should influence future decisions. To synthesize effectively, finance professionals must adopt the mindset of a storyteller. Every dataset tells a story about the business – its challenges, successes and potential future. By focusing on the narrative, you ensure that your presentation is not just a collection of numbers but a cohesive and compelling argument that informs and inspires action.

Ultimately, the goal is to move beyond simply reporting data to providing insights that drive strategic decision-making. When you synthesize rather than summarize, you elevate your role from an information provider to a trusted advisor who shapes the organization's future direction (Figure 5.4).

MOVING FROM INSIGHTS TO RECOMMENDATIONS

By implementing the ideas in this chapter, you have already significantly increased your value contribution by moving from presenting historical numbers to providing specific, targeted insights. You have helped your audience understand the 'what' and 'so what' of the data.

Figure 5.4 Summarizing vs. synthesizing.

At this point, your audience should realize the importance of the key attention points and be willing to do something to change the trajectory. However, having only just been introduced to the insights, your audience is unlikely to have an informed opinion about what to do about the situation. They are likely to ask 'then what?' to get your guidance on what needs to happen to improve the performance related to the topic. Whether presenting a challenge or an opportunity, you must be prepared to recommend the necessary steps to capitalize on the situation. This is covered by the third step of our communicative framework and the focus of the next chapter.

SARAH UNCOVERS THE ROOT CAUSES OF POOR REVENUE PERFORMANCE

Before Sarah starts uncovering the root causes of poor revenue performance to address the concerns highlighted by the CCO and what she has uncovered from her initial analysis, she returns to day two of her course on executive communication of financials. Here, she learns about the importance of

Step 2: Insights

insights, how to generate and present them and how to tailor the presentation to a specific audience.

She has already done the descriptive analysis, yet before she starts the diagnostic and predictive analysis she tries to put herself in the CCO's shoes. Here is her thought process as she goes through the seven questions.

1. **Who's is the audience?** The CCO.
2. **What must they do?** Increase revenue to close the gap in the budget.
3. **What do they see?** Lower than expected sales activity.
4. **What do they say?** The main issue is an unproductive sales force.
5. **What do they do?** Communicates to the sales force to increase productivity with an increasingly harsh rhetoric.
6. **What do they hear?** The sales force complains about too much administrative work, which prevents them from spending time with current and potential customers.
7. **What do they think and feel?** There is a growing frustration across the CCO organization, which, if unattended, could lead to laying off sales staff without increasing revenue, at least in the short term.

COMMUNICATING FINANCIALS TO EXECUTIVES

Now, Sarah can start her diagnostic analysis. She knows revenue is below budget, sales activity is below expectations and she has experienced firsthand the administrative burden the sales force faces. Having already fixed the potential root cause of the administrative burden Sarah is curious to see if the next month's sales activity is increasing. Unfortunately, that is not the case and it is back to the drawing board.

First she conducts a correlation analysis between sales activity and revenue. Here she identifies a relatively strong positive correlation with a three month delay. Hence, three months pass from the time the sales activity changes until the change is visible in the revenue. Using that insight she can now calculate how much sales activity is needed to hit the monthly revenue budget and what is required to fully bridge the gap to the annual budget.

Next she returns to the salespeople she spoke to initially to convey these insights. She asks them what must happen to increase the sales activity to the desired levels. They reveal to Sarah that it technically would be possible to conduct this many sales calls if they increased the ratio of virtual sales calls and equipped the sales force with tablets to register sales activity immediately after a sales call rather than having to return to the office.

However, more leads must be in the pipeline to meaningfully reach these activity levels. Sarah has

Step 2: Insights

access to the sales pipeline so this analysis is straightforward. She sees that sales activity could quickly increase above current levels; however, this would only close half the gap. As such, the leads to close the other half are missing.

Sarah is ready to synthesize the financial status and share the key attention points.

1. Sales activity has been low due to a high administrative workload caused by insufficient use of CRM system capabilities and weak sales processes.
2. To close the revenue gap to the budget, the sales force would need to increase sales activity significantly, by 55% compared to the previous six months.
3. Fixing the administrative issues would enable the sales force to increase their activity; however, they need leads to increase their activity to the required level.

Sarah suspects these are not the only issues to tackle to bridge the revenue gap to budget. However, it is enough to drive a meaningful discussion about what actions to take at the next monthly management meeting. We will check with Sarah to see how she gets along in the next chapter as she also prepares to make a recommendation.

CHAPTER SIX

STEP 3: RESOLUTION: WHAT CAN WE DO ABOUT IT?

Having isolated the main insights by asking 'so what?', it is time to ask the logical next question: 'Then what?' While the 'so what?' identifies why the finding is relevant to the audience, the 'then what?' identifies what they can do about it. In other words, the previous section outlined why the audience should care, and now we must present what they should do about it (Figure 6.1).

Too often, finance professionals present relevant information and key points of attention without proposing a potential way forward. The audience is left with information about the current financial situation

Figure 6.1 5-step financial communication framework – step 3.

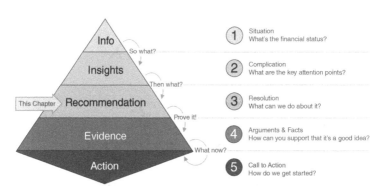

and potential main drivers but without guidance or advice on the decisions based on the input. Reflecting on the impact equation (Insights × Influence = Impact) presented earlier, by only providing insights you are neglecting the opportunity to influence decision-making by providing a clear recommendation. Moreover, you fail to create the intended impact.

In contrast, a skilled finance and data professional sees himself or herself as an equal business partner and takes responsibility for driving real business outcomes – not just providing an output. This entails having the courage to make decisions or recommend actions in the organization's best interests. It also means understanding that your insights are worth nothing if nobody does something differently. For insights to create impact, there needs to be execution.

Step 3: Resolution

A classical riddle goes: "Three birds sat on a fence. One decides to fly away. How many birds are still on the fence?" We are inclined to believe that the answer is two. However, that is not the case. All three birds remain on the fence. The decision to fly away is not an action. Moreover, just like the riddle, insights presented by finance professionals only create tangible business outcomes if someone is convinced to act as a result. A decision must be made and action must be taken. On its own, your Excel model is worth nothing. Even your colourful dashboard or extensive management report is worth very little if they do not spark action somewhere in the organization. An idea or insight is only as good as its execution.

DISTINGUISH BETWEEN OUTPUT AND OUTCOME

A good starting point when deciding what to recommend to management is the distinction between output and outcome. The output is the analysis (data model, calculations, etc.) and documentation (report, presentation, etc.), while the outcome is the resulting impact on the organization regarding decision-making processes and behavioral change.

COMMUNICATING FINANCIALS TO EXECUTIVES

That is, excellent finance and data professionals are concerned about their output – and the reports or analyses they deliver. They are concerned about the outcome – the decisions and actions resulting from understanding and accepting the presented insights. Consequently, recommendations should be made with the expected outcome in mind. Take a starting point in the data and insights focusing on recommendations that drive the desired business outcomes most effectively.

Unfortunately, measuring our success by the quality and accuracy of our outputs, such as detailed reports, polished Excel sheets and well-structured financial models, is more manageable. However, our deliverables have no inherent value – they only become valuable when used to make better and wiser decisions. Our success as finance professionals results from our impact on the organization's strategic choices and overall performance, not from the structure of our Excel model.

Imagine you have performed a product profitability analysis. You have calculated the individual profitability of different product groups by analyzing prices, cost of goods sold (COGS) and allocated overhead cost. You have presented a product profitability overview (Step 1 – Information) and highlighted that three particular product groups account

Step 3: Resolution

for an extraordinary contribution to the company's overall profitability (Step 2 – Insights). At this point, you could leave your output in the hands of others for them to decipher what to do about it. However, suppose you want to make sure that your efforts create a real impact on the organization. In that case, you must convince management to follow your recommendation to reallocate resources to increase marketing spend and production capacity to the profitable product lines (Step 3 – Recommendation). Keeping the desired outcome in mind maintains your focus on influencing the stakeholders to make smarter decisions, resulting in an increased bottom line. For other similar examples see Figure 6.2.

When distinguishing between output and outcome consider that we do not succeed in isolation. Instead, we succeed when we can indirectly influence results by enabling our business stakeholders to improve their performance.

Figure 6.2   From output to impact.

Output — The deliverables you create		Outcome — The way your output is used		Impact — The value created by the outcome
Profitability analysis	→	Resource reallocation	→	Increased bottom line
Variance analysis	→	Mitigating actions	→	Improved performance
Budget process	→	More accurate budget	→	Capital optimization

DARE TO HAVE
AN OPINION

Sometimes, finance professionals refrain from providing recommendations, feeling reluctant to share their opinions about business-related matters besides the numbers. For example, presenting a marketing spend reallocation based on the abovementioned profitability analysis to a Chief Commercial Officer might feel uncomfortable since it can be intrusive to his or her domain. Secondly, by presenting the recommendation, one might fear coming across as ignorant or even gullible by not knowing all the details about the commercial side of the business.

There is a valid point in ensuring you do not come across as patronizing or condescending when presenting your recommendations. So, do your homework and know your stakeholders' preferences before leaning out. However, experience from finance business partnering programs across a wide range of industries shows that business leaders, in general, crave more involvement from Finance in decision-making. As one senior commercial director put it: 'Finance must have the capacity to influence decisions, to participate and to challenge the status quo'. In most cases, business executives are eager to get data-driven input and recommendations from those who know the numbers the best.

Consequently, it is a mistake not to dare to have an informed opinion – and recommendation – about the actions to be taken based on the data and insights you have decided to present. Even if you do not have all the answers or understand all the details (nobody ever does), your opinion will likely be a valuable input to the overall decision-making process. After all, leadership always has the option to say no to what you are proposing.

This is not to say that you ought to use what consultants call the POOMA technique ('Pulled out of my ass'). However, often it is sufficient to use your analytical skills to conclude potential ways to resolve challenges or leverage opportunities presented to management. A proper combination of business acumen, industry insights and understanding of the numbers can easily be sufficient to form a relevant opinion about the actions to take.

That said, for very complex issues, it can be worth taking a more structured approach to identify relevant solutions to recommend. One way to organize your approach is to follow some basic principles of structured problem-solving.

LEVERAGE STRUCTURED PROBLEM-SOLVING

Convincing someone to act on your recommendations is easier said than done. However, showcasing that your recommendations are based on a structured problem-solving process creates credibility and makes it easier to convince your audience to act on your findings.

By leveraging structured problem-solving, you can dissect complex issues, identify underlying root causes and present actionable recommendations to your business counterparts. The easiest way to do so is to follow a straightforward, 3-step methodical approach:

1. Define the problem.
2. Disaggregate the problem.
3. Design the solution.

This '3D process' allows you to bridge the gap between raw financial data and strategic decision-making by going beyond simply reporting numbers to delivering recommendations that drive performance improvements and align financial outcomes with broader business objectives.

Step 3: Resolution

Define the Problem

Having presented the financial status and pinpointed specific insights, commence by considering the consequences associated with your findings. What is the problem (or opportunity) that needs to be addressed? We often mistakenly jump to conclusions when identifying a relevant outlier or trend in our data. This is a natural result of action bias – the psychological phenomenon where we favor action over inaction, even when there is no indication doing so would lead to a better result. Instead, you should fully understand the problem before you propose a solution. This entails staying explorative despite the initial urge to pursue the first and best idea that springs to mind.

Imagine you have presented the monthly variance analysis and the financial overview and highlighted extraordinary cost variances. Before recommending actions to mitigate the negative cost trends, ensure you fully understand the problem. Why is the cost variance a problem, and what are the consequences if nothing is done? Is this an urgent problem, or can it be handled over a longer period? There are many relevant questions to ask to understand the issue better.

Einstein is famously quoted as saying: 'If I had an hour to solve a problem and my life depended on the solution, I would spend the first 55 minutes determining the proper question to ask, for once I know the proper question, I could solve the problem in less than 5 minutes'. The point is that taking the time to uncover all relevant aspects of the problem before moving on will make it much easier to come up with the right solution. Consequently, it is time well invested to fully define and understand an issue before moving into solution mode. To do so, consider exploring key elements such as stakeholders, scope, resources, timing and success criteria.

- **Stakeholders:** Consider the stakeholders, including those who might cause the issue and those affected by it. These are the individuals or groups who are affected by or have an interest in the problem. Stakeholders can include internal departments, such as finance, sales or operations, and external parties, suppliers, customers or investors.
- **Scope:** Consider the full scope of the problem. The scope defines the boundaries of the issue, including what is included and what is excluded. Is the problem affecting a specific department, project or process? Or does it span multiple areas of the business? Clearly defining the scope prevents you from veering into unrelated issues or wasting resources on

Step 3: Resolution

areas outside the problem's influence. A clear scope also helps manage expectations with your audience by outlining what will be addressed and what will not.

- **Resources (including cost):** Every problem comes with resource constraints and understanding these upfront is crucial for developing realistic solutions. Resources can include personnel, financial budgets, data and technology. Consider the cost of solving the problem, whether it involves direct expenses like hiring consultants or indirect costs such as the time invested by internal teams. There will often be competing priorities for these resources, so you must assess whether the benefits of solving the problem justify the costs.
- **Timing:** Timing is another critical element in understanding and defining a problem. How urgent is the issue? Does it require an immediate solution or can it be addressed over a longer timeline? Defining the timing helps prioritize the problem relative to other business challenges. In fast-moving environments, delays in solving a problem can lead to escalating costs, lost opportunities or deteriorating stakeholder relationships. By setting clear timeframes, you can propose an achievable and realistic solution.

- **Success criteria:** Finally, define success criteria for when and how the problem will be solved. What does success look like for the stakeholders involved? In financial contexts, success criteria might include achieving specific cost reductions, improving cash flow or hitting profitability targets. Clear success criteria ensure that the solutions proposed are measurable and aligned with business goals. Without well-defined success metrics, assessing whether the problem has been resolved effectively or if further adjustments are needed becomes difficult.

In summary, to make relevant and data-backed recommendations you must fully understand and define the problem you are trying to solve.

Disaggregate the Problem

Having defined the problem, it is recommended that the issue be decomposed or disaggregated. This ensures that you solve not merely the visible symptoms but also the underlying root causes of the problem. The best recommendations you can make are those that solve the underlying root causes instead of just addressing the tip of the iceberg (Figure 6.3).

Step 3: Resolution

Figure 6.3 Symptoms vs. root causes.

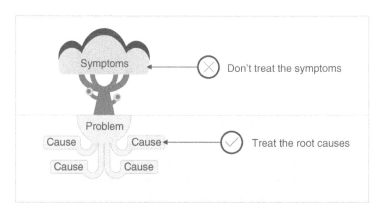

One particularly effective technique for decomposing problems and performing root-cause analysis is the 5× Why analysis. This straightforward approach involves asking 'Why?' five times (or as many times as needed) to peel back the layers of symptoms until the underlying cause is revealed (Figure 6.4).

By not stopping at surface-level symptoms, the 5× Why analysis helps you avoid jumping to conclusions or implementing short-term fixes. Instead, you ensure that you dig deeper into the factors driving the issue: process inefficiency, resource misallocation or a misalignment between financial goals and business strategy. This systematic approach ensures that the solutions proposed address the fundamental problem, leading to more sustainable, long-term improvements.

Figure 6.4 5× why.

Problem: Business unit has an unexpected overspend in the past quarter.

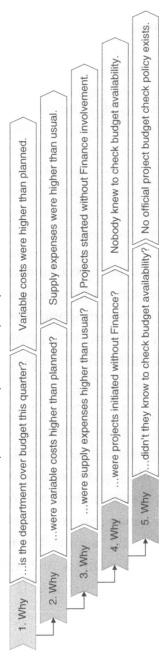

Solution: Create policy requiring budget checks when launching new projects.

Step 3: Resolution

When problems are complex, there is often more than one underlying cause. Declining cash flows can be caused simultaneously by ineffective sales and poor accounts receivable practices. For multiple root causes, it can be helpful to visualize your 5× Why analysis as a why-tree, a specific kind of logic tree (Figure 6.5).

Logic trees are visual tools that systematically break down complex problems or questions into smaller, manageable parts using a hierarchical structure. They are handy for structuring thinking, aiding analysis and driving problem-solving processes in an organized manner. Why-trees are diagnostic and help visualize the causality between different root causes and the overarching issue.

Gaining an overview of the various drivers of the issue makes it easier to form an informed opinion about how to address the problem. It also makes it easier to showcase that you have considered all aspects

Figure 6.5 A why tree.

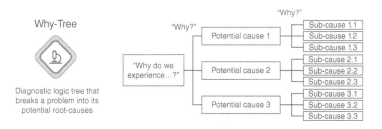

of the problem before presenting your recommendation. You ensure you know the details and do not just assume you do.

Design the Solution

As Einstein's quote exemplifies, spending adequate time understanding and decomposing the problem might make the preferable solution evident and easy to identify. However, in some cases, it can be helpful to complete another logic tree, focusing on solution exploration instead of root-cause identification. This is done by asking 'how?' instead of 'why?' to form what is known as a how-tree (Figure 6.6).

Where why-trees ensure that the root causes of problems are not overlooked, how-trees ensure that all possible solutions are considered once the problem is understood. The most effective paths are chosen to implement these solutions. As such, how-trees are prescriptive as opposed to the diagnostic why-trees.

Figure 6.6 A how tree.

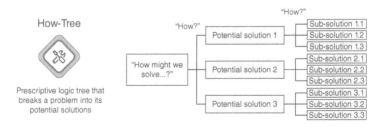

Step 3: Resolution

A benefit of the how-tree is that it forces you to develop competing solutions – different initiatives that could potentially resolve (or partially resolve) the same issue. You might increase sales by either launching a new marketing campaign or training the sales team. Both solutions are valid options addressing the same issue. Outlining such competing solutions options allows you to prioritize and ensure that you have a solid argumentation ready when management wants to understand your reasoning.

TIPS FOR MAKING A RECOMMENDATION

Whatever your recommendation, the goal remains to inform and inspire your executive audience to make better decisions that drive real business impact. This also means that you must be strategic about approaching it. Here are a couple of tips to ensure that your recommendation is well-received.

Prototype – Make Your Solution Visible

Creating a fast prototype is an effective way to visualize a proposed solution for management, enabling you to communicate a complex idea in a tangible and actionable manner. A prototype can be anything from a mock-up of a financial dashboard to a simplified version of a process improvement plan, and it should focus on key elements of the solution. By building a prototype, you offer management a preview of how the solution will function, its benefits and its potential impact. This visual representation fosters clarity and engagement, helping stakeholders grasp the practical implications of the solution more quickly than with verbal or written explanations alone. Fast prototypes also invite feedback early, allowing for adjustments and improvements before committing to full-scale implementation, ultimately enhancing decision-making and buy-in from leadership.

Present Options – There Is Never Just One Solution Option

Presenting solution options is invaluable when communicating with management, as it emphasizes collaboration and empowers decision-makers. Rather than prescribing a single course of action, offering multiple viable solutions acknowledges that there is rarely one perfect answer to a problem. This approach respects the diverse perspectives within the organization and recognizes that leadership should have a voice in choosing the path forward. Presenting options also fosters a sense of ownership and engagement, as management is involved in weighing the pros and cons of each option, whether based on cost, timing or strategic fit. By presenting options, you demonstrate that you have thoroughly considered different angles, making it easier for leaders to select a solution that aligns with the company's priorities.

Anticipate Objections – Be Ready with a Reply

Anticipating objections or potential questions from management is crucial to a successful presentation. When proposing a solution, you should consider the concerns that leadership might raise, such as cost, feasibility, alignment with strategic goals or the impact on other areas of the business. By preparing responses to these potential objections in advance, you are better equipped to address them proactively during the presentation, demonstrating thoroughness and foresight. This involves thinking from the management's perspective: What risks might they see? What data might they question? What trade-offs are involved? Preparing for these questions shows that the proposal has been well considered and helps foster a more productive dialogue. It builds trust by showing that all angles have been evaluated, leading to greater confidence in the solution and a smoother decision-making process.

SUPPORTING YOUR RECOMMENDATION WITH ARGUMENTS

Having defined your recommendation, you now must build a case for its validity by outlining a solid and structured argumentation. You cannot expect management to accept your recommendation without building a strong and fact-based case for the solution. This is covered by the fourth step of the communication process and the focus point of the next chapter.

SARAH IDEATES POTENTIAL SOLUTIONS

It is time for day 3 of Sarah's communication course and it could not have been timelier. She has uncovered the root cause of the poor revenue

Step 3: Resolution

performance: missing leads. She is unsure of what to do from here as if the solution was obvious it would probably already have been done.

On the course Sarah learns that it is natural for people in her role to think like that but becomes aware that old solutions could be just as viable as new and untested ones. That is because the context for trying a solution has changed. Hence, what did not work in the past could work today because of, for example, new technology or capabilities.

Sarah also gets challenged on her root cause analysis. Did she do a proper analysis or did she jump to conclusions by concluding that it is lack of leads? It could also be that the sales force is not adequately trained to run high-quality sales meetings that increase the conversion ratio. When she created her why-tree for her issue it was evident that it was not mutually exclusive and collectively exclusive (MECE) and she missed the other side of the solution space. Hence, before starting to shoot at the Chief Marketing Officer for lack of leads, it is essential that she also speaks to the sales staff, their managers and perhaps even some of the customers to learn about the quality of the sales dialogues. For now, she stays with the initial hypothesis that the lack of leads is causing poor revenue performance. To generate solution ideas, she completes a how-tree, which you can see here (Figure 6.7).

Figure 6.7 An example of a how tree.

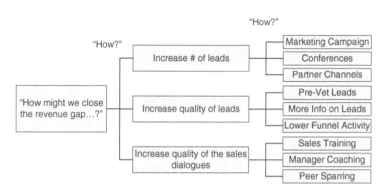

This provided Sarah with two tracks to explore. (1) Increase the number of leads and (2) increase the quality of the leads.

- **Increase the number of leads:** There are no silver bullets here and the company frequently runs marketing campaigns so naturally Sarah could investigate the effectiveness of these. Secondly, she has spoken to a few team members who occasionally speak at conferences and they all say that what leads they collect is limited. However, a new idea came to the table: developing partner channels. By leveraging other companies in the industry that have the same customer base but offer non-competing solutions there could be a way of engaging them to generate new leads.

Step 3: Resolution

- **Increase the quality of the leads:** Sarah has learned from some of the salespeople that they would often waste time on leads with no interest and buying power. This was another contributing factor to their perceived inefficiency. Hence, Sarah wanted to explore ways to increase the quality of the leads. This could be done by establishing a contact centre to pre-vet the leads before they were funneled to the salespeople. Another option would be to collect more information on the leads through expanded contact forms etc., for salespeople to better judge whether a lead was worth the time. Finally, conducting lower funnel activities like webinars, events, etc., could also be possible.

Sarah presents her how-tree to a group of salespeople she has been in close dialogue with throughout her investigations. Together, they decide that the most significant potential lies in the partner channels and lower funnel activities that could be conducted in collaboration with the new partners. Before presenting the ideas she must back them up with good arguments. In the next chapter, we will check in with Sarah to uncover how she does that and prepares to present her recommendation.

CHAPTER SEVEN

STEP 4: ARGUMENTATION: WHY IS THIS A GOOD IDEA?

Having presented your recommendation, you must now prove why your proposed solution is the right option for management. Even if your idea seems reasonable at first glance, you are unlikely to encounter a management team willing to take your suggestions at face value. You must build a robust and coherent argumentation to support your idea (Figure 7.1).

Figure 7.1 5-step financial communication framework – step 4.

THE DIFFERENCE BETWEEN ARGUMENT AND FACTS

Understanding the distinction between arguments and facts is crucial to delivering a compelling recommendation that convinces management to act. Both play different yet complementary roles in shaping the recommendation and persuading decision-makers. The key lies in integrating facts and arguments to build a strong, coherent case.

Facts: The Foundation of Trust

Facts are the objective, verifiable data points that form the foundation of any recommendation.

Step 4: Argumentation

In finance, these might include revenue figures, profitability ratios, cost structures and market trends. Facts are undisputed truths, that is, numbers, results or events that can be backed up by reliable sources such as financial statements, industry benchmarks or market reports. Management will expect to see facts because they lend credibility. However, while facts are necessary, they are rarely sufficient. A management team is not just looking for what the numbers say but what those numbers mean in the context of your recommendation. This is where arguments come into play.

Arguments: The Art of Persuasion

Arguments go beyond stating facts: they involve interpreting facts, creating logical connections and linking them to your recommendation. An argument presents why a particular course of action should be taken and how the facts support that decision. For example, simply stating that profit margins have decreased by 5% is a fact. However, you are constructing a persuasive argument when you argue that this margin decline results from rising supplier costs, coupled with insufficient pricing adjustments, and propose renegotiating contracts or introducing cost-saving measures. Here, the facts (declining margins and rising costs) support your argument for a strategic response.

The Interplay of Facts and Arguments

In your recommendation to management, facts provide the solid base that gives your arguments credibility. However, to be persuasive you must bridge those facts with a narrative explaining why they are important and what should be done. Without facts, your argument will lack substance. Without arguments, your facts may seem disconnected or irrelevant.

Famous data scientist W. Edwards Deming said *'Without data you are just another person with an opinion'*.

This is true – you must back your arguments with data to ensure data-driven decision-making. However, the alternative statement, 'Without an opinion, you are just another person with data', is also true. You cannot rely on data alone. You must lean out and dare to articulate an informed opinion about the data to convince others to act on it.

Thus, differentiating between facts and arguments and then intertwining them effectively is essential for any financial communication aimed at management.

Step 4: Argumentation

Grounding your arguments in facts builds trust and credibility. Constructing persuasive arguments helps management make informed decisions that drive the organization forward.

Here are two examples of the interplay between fact, interpretation and argument. The example shows how the argument proposes a course of action based on facts and interpretations to showcase a persuasive and specific path forward.

Fact: 'Our company's operating expenses have increased by 15% over the past year, primarily due to higher raw material costs'.

Interpretation: 'If this trend continues, our profit margins will shrink by another 2% by year-end, putting additional pressure on our bottom line'.

Argument: 'To mitigate this risk, we should explore alternative suppliers with lower costs or renegotiate contracts with our current suppliers. Implementing cost-saving measures could result in an estimated 8% reduction in operating expenses within the next two quarters'.

Fact: 'Our customer satisfaction score has declined by 10% over the past quarter, mainly due to longer response times from customer support.'

Interpretation: 'If this downward trend continues, it may result in a loss of customer loyalty and a potential decrease in repeat purchases.'

Argument: 'To counter this risk, we should consider implementing a streamlined ticketing system or additional training for our support team. Addressing response time issues could help restore customer satisfaction, potentially boosting retention rates within the next six months.'

THE MAGIC NUMBER OF THREE: WHY THREE ARGUMENTS ARE IDEAL

In communication, particularly when persuading management, simplicity and clarity are key. Presenting three arguments to support your recommendation is one of the most effective techniques to enhance clarity and impact. This concept, often referred to as 'the magic number of three', is rooted in both psychology and communication theory, and it plays a crucial role in ensuring your message is clear, memorable and convincing.

Step 4: Argumentation

The Psychology Behind the Number Three

There is a reason why the number three resonates with human cognition. Our brains are wired to perceive and process information in patterns, and three is the smallest number needed to form a pattern. This is why the 'rule of three' is prevalent in various aspects of communication, from storytelling to public speaking. It works because:

1. **Three is simple:** It provides enough content to be substantive but not overwhelming. The human brain can easily retain and recall three distinct points.
2. **Three creates balance:** Presenting two arguments might seem too weak or incomplete, while presenting four or more may overload your audience with information. Three strikes the perfect balance between brevity and depth.
3. **Three is persuasive:** A trio of arguments builds a rhythm and cadence that feels complete and comprehensive. This helps create a compelling narrative without over-complicating the message.

Furthermore, the 'rule of three' plays to the strengths of a powerful mnemonic technique called 'chunking' (Miller, 1994). The technique involves grouping individual pieces of information into manageable units, or 'chunks', to improve memory retention and comprehension. Chunking is why phone numbers are often presented with spacing like '1512 5555 1212' instead of '151255551212'. The human brain perceives the first version as three numbers, '1512', '5555', and '1212', which is easier to remember than the 12 unique values in the second version even if the data are the same.

When presenting financials to management, chunking helps aggregate numerous data points into three cohesive, digestible arguments. This method simplifies complex information and enhances clarity by structuring facts in a way that is easier for the audience to process. Using chunking, you can ensure that key messages stand out, making your recommendation more memorable and persuasive while avoiding information overload.

Three Arguments to Convince Management

Framing your case around three strong arguments enhances persuasiveness when presenting your recommendation to management and presenting three arguments forces you to distill your message into the most critical and impactful points. It ensures that each argument is relevant and directly supports your recommendation, removing the noise and focusing on what truly matters.

Step 4: Argumentation

Furthermore, senior executives are often faced with numerous decisions and limited time. Structuring your case around three key arguments increases the likelihood that they will remember your points. Three key arguments are a manageable number that allows them to walk away with a clear understanding of the reasoning behind your recommendation. Finally, you create a sense of completeness and authority by presenting three arguments. With each argument building on the last, you progressively strengthen your case. This creates momentum that encourages management to act on your recommendation (Figure 7.2).

Each argument is distinct and relevant and reinforces the recommendation in this example. Each argument builds on the previous one, creating a well-rounded case that addresses immediate concerns, offers a clear solution and aligns with long-term strategic goals. By providing three compelling arguments,

Figure 7.2 Argument tree.

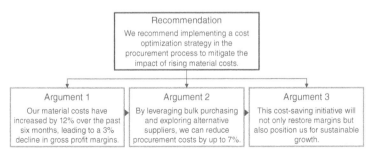

you create a structured, memorable and persuasive narrative that resonates with management, making your recommendation more likely to lead to action.

EXPANDING THE DEFINITION OF FACTS BEYOND NUMBERS

When constructing your argumentation, it is easy to assume that facts must always be numerical – sales figures, profit margins or cost reductions. After all, this is the comfort zone of most data and finance professionals. However, facts encompass much more than just numbers. They can include a variety of evidence forms that provide credibility and support for your arguments, such as expert statements, customer testimonials and industry research. These non-numerical facts can be as powerful as data points in building a compelling case for your recommendation.

Expert Statements

Expert statements can add a layer of authority and legitimacy to your argument. When an industry leader, consultant or internal subject-matter expert

Step 4: Argumentation

weighs in on a situation, their opinion is seen as credible because it is grounded in their experience and knowledge. For example, if you recommend investing in a new technology, citing an expert opinion on why this technology is vital for maintaining a competitive edge can solidify your argument. Experts bring specialized knowledge that management may not have, helping them to make informed decisions.

Example: *'According to Gartner's recent report, companies that implement AI in their finance functions can expect efficiency gains of up to 25% over the next five years'.*

This expert-backed fact strengthens your case by highlighting external validation and industry-wide trends that align with your recommendation.

Customer Testimonials

Customer feedback is another piece of factual evidence, mainly when recommendations involve customer-facing initiatives. Testimonials and case studies can reveal a decision's real-world impact, providing qualitative proof of the effectiveness of a particular strategy. If you recommend a shift in customer engagement or product offerings, showcasing how these changes have positively impacted

COMMUNICATING FINANCIALS TO EXECUTIVES

similar companies or sharing testimonials from satisfied clients adds a relatable human element to your argument. Management often finds such insights valuable because they reflect market sentiment and real-world results directly.

Example: 'Our top customer, who generates 15% of our revenue, recently shared that faster delivery times would significantly increase their annual purchase volume with us'.

In this case, the customer's statement provides a fact that complements financial data and demonstrates the potential for revenue growth.

Industry Research

Research and reports from reputable sources such as industry white papers, market analyses or economic forecasts are other valuable facts that can support your arguments. These sources provide a broader context for management to view the recommendation and make data-driven decisions aligned with market trends or future forecasts. For instance, if you propose a strategic expansion into a new market, citing relevant research on market demand, growth projections or competitor activity provides a factual basis for why the expansion is a smart business move.

Step 4: Argumentation

Example: *'According to McKinsey's latest industry report, the global market for digital payment solutions is expected to grow by 30% over the next three years, representing a key opportunity for our business to expand'.*

This fact highlights external trends that management can use to gauge the validity of your recommendation.

Integrating Non-Numerical Facts with Financial Data

While numbers are essential in financial communication, integrating non-numerical facts such as expert opinions, customer feedback and industry research can provide a richer, more compelling narrative. These facts often add context and nuance to the hard data, helping management understand your recommendation's quantitative and qualitative aspects. By expanding your definition of facts to include these forms of evidence, you build a more persuasive and well-rounded argument, increasing the likelihood that your recommendation will resonate with management and lead to actionable decisions.

THE IMPORTANCE OF SELECTIVITY

When presenting a recommendation to management, the arguments you choose to include can make or break the effectiveness of your message. While it might be tempting to overwhelm your audience with data and analysis, successful communication often adheres to the 'less is more' principle. Being selective with your arguments ensures you focus on the most impactful and relevant points, delivering a clear, concise and compelling recommendation.

Why Selectivity Matters

Management's time and attention are limited. In an environment where leaders constantly make high-stakes decisions, presenting a barrage of information can backfire. Irrelevant data points or extraneous arguments only cause confusion, dilute your message and potentially obscure the actual value of your recommendation. Effective communication, especially when dealing with financials, demands that you cut through the noise and present only what is necessary to drive home your key points.

The strength of a recommendation lies not in the quantity of supporting arguments but in the quality and relevance of those arguments. Thus, you should ensure that each argument serves a distinct purpose, directly supporting the primary recommendation. Anything that does not serve this purpose should be left out. Data or points only loosely connected to the recommendation weakens the overall case, distracts management from the core message and leaves them questioning what is truly important. Furthermore, streamline your argument by stripping away unnecessary details. Doing so ensures that your three arguments work cohesively to build a compelling and logical narrative that is easy to follow.

How to Select the Right Three Arguments

When deciding which three arguments to include, focus on relevance, impact and simplicity. Here is how you can approach the selection process:

Relevance: Ask yourself: *Does this argument directly support the decision I want management to make?* If not, it is likely to be irrelevant. Each argument should be laser-focused on your recommendation, avoiding tangential points that could distract from your main message.

Impact: Not all facts or arguments carry equal weight. Choose the three arguments that will most impact management's decision. These should be the most compelling, backed by solid evidence or data, and likely to resonate with management's strategic priorities. Consider your audience and their priorities when selecting the arguments.

Simplicity: An argument might be valid, but it risks losing the audience if it is too complex or convoluted. Consequently, you should prioritize simplicity by selecting three straightforward and easy-to-explain arguments. Complex or overly technical points may distract management, leading them to miss the essence of your recommendation.

In conclusion, the strength of your recommendation lies in your ability to be selective. Focusing on three relevant, impactful simple arguments ensures your message is clear and persuasive. Avoid including unnecessary data points or overly complex arguments that could distract from your main objective. Remember, less is more when it comes to effective communication. Stripping away the excess allows your essential points to shine through.

Step 4: Argumentation

FROM ARGUMENT TO DECISION

Presenting a solid argument will increase your likelihood of convincing management. However, thousands of management meetings have been held where an apparent agreement never led to any subsequent action or real impact on the organization. Convincing your audience about your idea is not enough. You need to convince them to act on it. This is the topic of the next chapter and the communicative framework's final step.

SARAH BACKS UP HER RECOMMENDATION

With a group of salespeople Sarah has decided that the best path to closing the revenue gap to budget will be to open a new partnership sales channel and conduct lower funnel activities. Before Sarah can present this path forward she needs to form it into a recommendation and back it up with arguments. Here is Sarah's recommendation.

"We suggest opening a new sales channel in the form of partnerships with other industry players and

jointly conducting lower funnel activities to develop quality leads that will help us close our revenue gap to budget before the end of the year".

There are two questions that Sarah needs to answer to back up her recommendation.

- Why is opening a new sales channel with partners a good idea compared to other available options?
- How will joint lower funnel activities help to develop higher quality leads?

Sarah learned on her training course that she needs three arguments and so she set out to do some further research. The initial hypothesis was that using partnerships was the best solution because it would be a brand-new sales channel the company had not used before.

During her research she uncovers some tangible benefits: (1) strong partnership programs contribute on average to 28% of a company's revenue and (2) strong partnership programs help companies double the revenue growth rate. She also discusses leveraging partnerships with the salespeople and learns that many have worked with partner programs in previous companies. That means they already have the experience to work with partnerships. Finally, the salespeople already have many ideas for lower funnel activities,

Step 4: Argumentation

such as joint account-based marketing and co-hosted webinars and events.

Sarah already discussed alternatives to increasing the number of leads and the quality of the leads when she created the how-tree with the salespeople. They did not much discuss the opportunity to increase the quality of the sales dialogue as this was a more sensitive topic. It would imply that the salespeople were not good enough at their job. However, she already knows that the CCO has questioned the quality of the dialogue. She would therefore need to have this option available as an alternative solution but also have arguments in place to show why the recommendation is the better option.

Going through training herself to develop her communication skills, Sarah knows that it takes a long time to become good at what you're learning and the revenue gap to budget is becoming an urgent problem. Therefore, training could be a good, longer-term solution to ensure Solara Tech does not face the same challenges next year. She will thus highlight it as an alternative that can be activated once the other activities are up and running and showing results.

CHAPTER EIGHT

STEP 5: HOW DO WE GET STARTED?

Your audience is now hooked on your idea. They understand the challenges, the proposed solution and the arguments. Now, you need to facilitate a decision to move forward with implementation. You must support the transition from presentation to decision and decision to action (Figure 8.1).

SUMMARIZE AND ENSURE A COMMON UNDERSTANDING

Before you jump into practical planning for implementing your proposed solution, taking adequate time to summarize what was discussed is often relevant. At this point, your audience has received much

Figure 8.1   5-step financial communication framework – step 5.

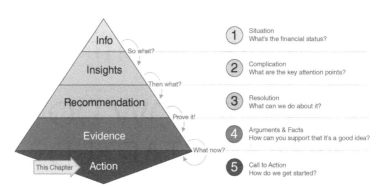

information and might be stretching their mental capacity to follow the train of thought. You might think the logic and narrative are sound but remember that this is likely the first time your audience is presented with the information. To ensure that your audience digests the information this is the optimal time to give them time to reflect, and to provide feedback and relevant input. Facilitate a dialogue to ensure that everyone is on the same page.

ANTICIPATE CHANGE RESISTANCE

When facilitating a discussion around your recommendation, it is helpful to anticipate potential questions in advance. It is natural for people to resist change when new ways of working are proposed, and any strong recommendation will likely involve altering existing processes. Even senior management, accustomed to driving and adapting to change, may initially experience resistance when confronted with new ideas.

The SCARF Model – Sources of Change Resistance

One practical framework for understanding and addressing change resistance is the SCARF model (Figure 8.2), developed by David Rock (Rock and Ringleb, 2013). SCARF stands for Status, Certainty, Autonomy, Relatedness and Fairness – five social domains that, when threatened, can trigger resistance or defensiveness. Understanding these domains can help you foresee the emotional and psychological factors that may influence how your audience perceives your recommendation, allowing you to address concerns proactively.

1. **Status**

    The concept of status refers to how people perceive their standing or importance relative to others. A recommendation that may shift roles, alter responsibilities or impact hierarchy could be perceived as a threat to an individual's status. For example, if your recommendation suggests reallocating resources that might diminish

Figure 8.2 The SCARF model.

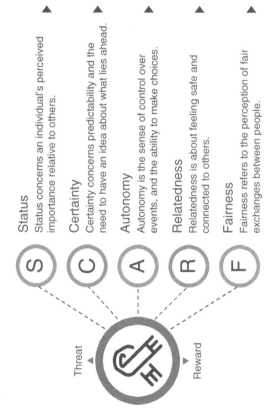

someone's influence, they may instinctively resist. To mitigate this, frame your proposal to emphasize opportunities for growth or improvement in status rather than potential losses.

Tip: Highlight how the change could enhance the status of those involved – perhaps by positioning them as key drivers of a strategic initiative or champions of a new, beneficial process.

2. **Certainty**

Certainty deals with people's need for predictability and understanding of the future. A recommendation that introduces ambiguity or disrupts familiar processes may create anxiety or resistance due to the perceived loss of control over outcomes. To reduce uncertainty, provide as much clarity as possible about your recommendation's implications, timeline and expected results.

Tip: Offer a clear roadmap and outline the steps for implementation, setting realistic expectations to give your audience a sense of security and predictability.

3. **Autonomy**

Autonomy is the perception of control over one's decisions and environment. If your recommendation appears to limit options, constrain decision-making or reduce flexibility, it may be met with pushback from those who feel their autonomy is being compromised.

To counter this, emphasize how the proposed change allows for individual choice or enhances overall decision-making.

Tip: Where possible, include options within the implementation process or provide opportunities for input, helping those affected by the change to feel that they are part of the decision rather than imposing it upon them.

4. **Relatedness**

Relatedness concerns the sense of belonging and connection to others. Changes that disrupt existing team dynamics, relationships or collaborative networks may trigger resistance. If your recommendation is perceived as creating silos, reducing interaction or alienating certain groups, people may feel a social disconnect. To address this, focus on how the change will foster collaboration, strengthen relationships or create a more inclusive environment.

Tip: Frame the recommendation to build stronger connections across teams or enhance the organization's shared sense of purpose.

5. **Fairness**

Fairness is the perception of being treated justly and equitably. If your recommendation favors certain groups, departments or individuals, it may generate feelings of injustice and lead to opposition. To preempt this, ensure

Step 5: How Do We Get Started?

transparency in decisions and how outcomes will be distributed.

Tip: Be transparent about how the benefits of the change will be shared across the organization and explain the rationale behind critical decisions to reinforce a sense of fairness.

By applying the SCARF model before your presentation, you can identify potential sources of resistance and consider ways to proactively address them or form relevant replies to management's inquiries. For instance, if you anticipate concerns about status or fairness, you can frame your recommendation to highlight opportunities for all stakeholders. If certainty and autonomy are at risk, providing clear timelines and options for input can make it easier for the audience to accept your proposal. Ultimately, the SCARF model equips you to present your case in a way that is not only logical but also empathetic, fostering greater acceptance and buy-in from management.

PAVE THE WAY FORWARD

After allowing reflection, you must conclude your presentation by clearly paving the way forward. While your audience may accept your recommendation, it is up to you to guide them on how to implement it effectively. Make it easy for them to take the next step – from decision to action. Present a clear plan, outline the tangible next steps and demonstrate that you have anticipated potential risks. Doing so ensures that the execution path is straightforward and actionable. One effective way to outline what is needed for implementation is to apply the project triangle (Rudder, Main and Watts, 2024) (Figure 8.3) considering the key elements of time, cost, scope and quality:

- **Time:** Clearly define the timeline for implementation, highlighting critical milestones and deadlines. This helps your audience understand the urgency and sequence of activities required,

Figure 8.3 The project triangle.

Step 5: How Do We Get Started?

making the process feel more manageable and structured.

- **Cost:** Present a realistic budget for the recommended change, including expected costs and potential savings. Transparency about the financial implications reassures stakeholders that resources have been considered and that the project is financially viable.

- **Scope:** Articulate the project's scope, detailing what will be covered and what is outside the implementation's boundaries. Being precise about the scope helps prevent misunderstandings and sets clear expectations for what the recommendation will achieve.

- **Quality:** Address how quality will be maintained throughout the implementation. Describe any standards or benchmarks needed and how you plan to monitor and ensure that the outcome aligns with organizational expectations.

By integrating these elements of the project triangle, you provide a comprehensive view of what it takes to implement your recommendation. It adds depth to your presentation and reinforces your readiness to support the change and navigate the complexities of moving from decision to action.

COMMUNICATING FINANCIALS TO EXECUTIVES

INSIST ON A DECISION: TURNING DISCUSSION INTO ACTION

When presenting to management, it is not enough to deliver compelling arguments and outline a path forward – you must also insist on a decision. Ensuring that your presentation concludes with a clear outcome is critical, as too many well-intentioned management meetings result in extensive discussions but ultimately fall short of real change. Even when great ideas are explored and potential strategies debated, the absence of a definitive decision often means those ideas fail to materialize into concrete actions.

The importance of driving a decision is twofold:

1. **Avoiding decision paralysis:** Management discussions often lead to insights, new ideas and thorough analysis, but without a decisive outcome, all that effort remains theoretical. Decision paralysis can occur when the group fails to commit due to a desire for more information, differing opinions or simply the comfort of staying in the status quo. As the presenter, you are responsible for

Step 5: How Do We Get Started?

steering the conversation towards a firm resolution.

2. **Ensuring accountability and momentum:** By securing a decision at the end of your presentation, you create a sense of accountability and urgency. It moves the recommendation from 'consideration' to an actionable 'commitment'. A clear decision creates momentum, helping to drive the implementation plan forward and signaling to all stakeholders that change is not just an option – it is the path that has been chosen.

To facilitate a decision, explicitly ask for a decision before wrapping up your presentation. Phrases like 'Can we agree to move forward with this plan?' or 'Are we ready to commit to the next steps?' ensure that the discussion culminates in a definitive conclusion. Furthermore, clarifying what will happen immediately after making a decision is essential. Outline the initial actions, who will be responsible and the immediate timeline. This reinforces that the decision is not just about agreement but about setting things in motion.

Consider again the tale about three birds sitting on a fence. One decides to fly away. How many birds are left on the fence? We are prone to think that only two birds are left on the fence. However, the decision to fly away is not the action. All birds remain on the fence until the real behavioral change happens. In the same way, you must make sure that you get a commitment to action – someone must do something different based on the decision to create a real impact.

Remember, inaction is a decision in itself – often the wrong one. Opportunities to improve, streamline processes or capitalize on market shifts are lost when decisions linger without commitment. Your role is to ensure that discussions lead to real-world impact by emphasizing the urgency and importance of moving from debate to action. By insisting on a decision, you transform ideas into tangible results, turning good management meetings into catalysts for meaningful change.

This concludes our walkthrough of the five-step model for communicating financials to executives. Completing all these steps for every financial presentation may seem daunting. However, once you start using the framework, it will become easier over time, and your impact as a finance professional will grow exponentially. We will share more tips on how to put it all together in a presentation in the subsequent chapters so you can learn how to become an excellent communicator of financials from end to end.

Step 5: How Do We Get Started?

GETTING STARTED WITH THE NEW SALES CHANNEL

The analysis is done, and the recommendation is ready, but Sarah knows it does not mean the work is done. That is due to the simple fact that decision ≠ action. Sarah needs to outline the implementation plan and immediate next steps and ensure accountability is assigned with relevant deadlines.

The implementation plan must be brief as results must be seen in the short term. The first step would be to identify relevant channel partners and contact them to book an initial meeting to discuss the potential and mutual benefits. From those meetings a recommendation of channel partners should be presented to the CCO for a decision. Once the channel partner(s) have been selected a planning meeting should occur to explore and agree on joint account-based marketing activities including co-hosted webinars and events. Sarah suggests setting a target for the first joint activities conducted three months after the recommendation is approved.

The first action to identify channel partners is assigned to the Head of Sales Channels, as she would be responsible for this new sales channel. This activity

COMMUNICATING FINANCIALS TO EXECUTIVES

should be completed within a week and meetings should be booked and take place in the coming three weeks. At the end of the third week a workshop is planned to recommend partners to work with. Sarah will propose herself as the project manager despite this not being a finance project, but she would like to see this through and thinks her work with the sales-people over the past months has given her much credibility with the team to take on this task.

The preparation for the meeting still needs to be completed. Sarah knows she needs to anticipate resistance to her recommendation and is considering the SCARF model to prepare for the meeting.

- **Status:** Since the recommendation addresses a key challenge of the CCO and proposes something the company has not done before Sarah does not expect the CCO to feel a loss of status should the recommendation be approved.
- **Certainty:** As this idea is new, there is less certainty that it will yield the expected results. However, a firm implementation plan backed by external data makes it a viable idea that on its own could close the entire revenue gap to budget.
- **Autonomy:** Sarah has been very inclusive in her analysis process involving many salespeople. However, she knows she must clarify the idea with the Head of Sales Channels before

presenting the recommendation. She also provides an alternative to her proposal: to increase the quality of the sales dialogue should management not like the recommendation.

- **Relatedness:** Sarah knows many of the salespeople have already worked with partners as a sales channel so the solution is familiar to them. With Sarah proposing herself as the project manager she thinks they will be comfortable moving ahead despite it being a new approach for Solara Tech.
- **Fairness:** This could easily have been Sarah's main challenge since she works in Finance and is proposing solutions for Sales. However, due to her inclusive process she has no significant concerns with fairness. The CCO and commercial leadership team should make and support the decision.

Sarah has never felt more prepared for a presentation even considering the potential change resistance. Now all that is left is to deliver the presentation.

It's Time to Present

It is exam time! Not in Sarah's training course but in the monthly management meeting. Sarah has rehearsed her presentation because she knows she

COMMUNICATING FINANCIALS TO EXECUTIVES

has to put in the extra effort to get her recommendation across.

- **Financials status:** She starts by highlighting that Solara Tech's financial status is US$5 million behind budget with six months left to close the gap.
- **Key attention points:** The main challenge is that too few sales calls are conducted and even if more calls could be conducted there would not be enough leads in the pipeline to close the gap. She has already worked with the salespeople to free up the capacity to perform more sales calls by removing administrative tasks.
- **What can we do about it?** That leaves the issue of a lack of leads for which Sarah recommends developing a partner sales channel and conducting joint lower-funnel activities.
- **How do we know it is a good idea?** Sarah cites external research showing that once the program is established the partner channel would more than close the gap to budget. However, as half the year has passed and it will take some time to get the solution off the ground the full effect is expected only next year.
- **How do we get started?** Sarah has outlined a clear implementation plan The following steps for the coming three weeks involve identifying

new partners, meeting with them and organizing a workshop to make recommendations.

The management team was amazed by Sarah's presentation as they had not seen her communicate in this way before. They are excited about the recommendation and the prospect of closing the revenue gap to budget. They are slightly concerned with the timeline but agree to put significant resources at Sarah's disposal to run the project. Sarah is very pleased with herself and is equally excited to get started. She reflects on her journey of becoming better at communicating financials to executives and is amazed by her progress. This approach will undoubtedly revolutionize her impact and career success, and the same could happen to you if you try it out!

CHAPTER NINE

CONSIDERATIONS ON DATA VISUALIZATIONS

When dealing with finance professionals as part of learning and development programs, Christian likes to compare the client's CFO to Indiana Jones – the iconic fictional character (Dykes, 2020). This usually sparks a heated debate about similarities and differences as the audience tries to identify the logic behind the comparison. Christian then continues to argue that all business-oriented finance professionals bear a resemblance to Indiana Jones. The reasoning is as follows.

Imagine yourself as the Indiana Jones of the business world. Just like the iconic archeologist, you embark on journeys to uncover hidden treasures buried deep within vast landscapes – except instead of ancient artifacts you search for actionable insights hidden within data. As an explorer you navigate through the labyrinth of financial figures, trends and patterns, armed with the latest tools and methodologies. However, your mission does not end with discovery. Like Indiana Jones you are also a professor, translating your findings for an audience eager to understand their significance.

The task is twofold: first, dig into the data and uncover the 'relics' – the key insights that will drive decision-making. Second, these findings must be clearly and convincingly communicated to an executive audience that may not speak the language of finance (Figure 9.1). It is not enough to find valuable insights; they must be presented in a way that resonates with executives who often crave clarity, simplicity and compelling visual narratives over intricate spreadsheets and technical jargon.

This process will be significantly easier if you follow the process outlined in previous chapters.

Figure 9.1 ROI vs. time/effort.

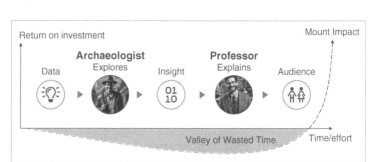

Considerations on Data Visualizations

However, even great insights and a well-structured top-down narrative aligned with our communicative framework will not always be sufficient to influence your executive audience. Moreover, if you fail in the role of professor – explaining the importance of your insights – you end up in what Christian refers to as the Valley of Wasted Time. This is where much time and resources have been invested in finding, cleaning and analyzing data. However, nobody uses the output for better decision-making or behavioral changes. No real business impact is created.

This chapter will explore how effective data visualization can help bridge the gap between exploration and explanation by supporting your narrative. We will see how proper data visualization techniques can support your narrative to influence your audience to act effectively based on your insights. By doing this, you ensure that you travel out of the Valley of Wasted Time and climb up the steep slope of Mount Impact.

MAKE IT EASY TO DECODE YOUR KEY MESSAGE

When presenting to executives you fight for their attention in an increasingly busy work environment. This fight is easy to lose, a problem which has been shown by recent studies that the average human attention span is decreasing. According to a study by Microsoft, people generally lose attention after 8.25 seconds – down from 12 seconds in the year 2000. This means that most humans now have an attention span shorter than that of the notoriously ill-focused goldfish, who manages to stay focused for nine seconds (McSpadden, 2015).

Attention span, the duration an individual can focus on a given task, activity or stimulus, is a critical component of cognitive functioning, directly affecting how we learn, work and engage with our environment. Various factors influence an individual's attention span, including age, gender, health, stress levels and environmental distractions. Executives often experience heightened stress and numerous distractions, significantly diminishing their ability to maintain focus. Consequently, to succeed in influencing executives you must make it as easy as possible to decode your message and translate your recommendations into action. After all, you effectively present to a goldfish – at least in attention span. Try decoding the visual in Figure 9.2.

If you are like most people, you will read the four sentences in the correct order without necessarily knowing why. Your attention is drawn to each

Figure 9.2 Visual decoding test.

sentence in the correct order. This works because the visual was created with the brain in mind, leveraging relevant techniques in size and colouring to guide your attention to the different elements.

In the same way you must support your narrative with great data visualizations that guide your executive audience's attention to the essential messages first, making it easy to decode the message.

SYSTEM 1 AND SYSTEM 2 THINKING

A good starting point when considering how to make your message easy to decode is to consider the two modes of thinking – System 1 and System 2 – as described by Daniel Kahneman, in his book *Thinking, Fast and Slow*. This theory was briefly introduced in a previous chapter, but let's consider the implications in relation to how our brains perceive data visualizations. (Kahneman, 2011) (Figure 9.3).

System 1 is fast, intuitive and automatic. It is the brain's default mode, making quick judgments based on experience and patterns. It is efficient but often relies on mental shortcuts, sometimes at the expense of deep analysis. In contrast, **System 2** is slow, deliberate and analytical. It is responsible for complex

Figure 9.3 System 1 vs. system 2 thinking.

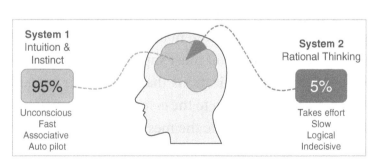

problem-solving, rational thinking and careful evaluation. However, engaging System 2 requires significantly more mental energy and effort, and as a result it tends to be activated sparingly – only when the brain deems it necessary.

Executives often face a barrage of information and must make decisions rapidly. While System 2 thinking is crucial for complex, high-stakes decisions, engaging this mode for every choice is impractical and exhausting. This means that, as a finance professional, you must aim to craft your presentations and visualizations in a way that allows your audience to make quick yet accurate decisions using System 1 thinking.

Designing for System 1: Presenting Insights Clearly and Effectively

To optimize for System 1 thinking, focus on making your insights easy to digest. Use intuitive, compelling visuals and quickly convey the main point. A well-designed chart or infographic should be immediately understandable, allowing executives to grasp the critical message immediately. Use colour, shape and layout strategically to draw attention to key takeaways and trends, ensuring that the eye is guided to the most critical information first.

Engaging System 2 When Necessary

While most decisions can be made using System 1 thinking, there will be instances when you need your audience to engage in deeper analysis. This is where System 2 thinking becomes valuable. However, given the cognitive effort required, guiding the audience gently into this mode is crucial. Structure your presentation from simple to more complex points, giving clear signposts when a deeper dive is needed. Use storytelling techniques and frame complex data within a narrative that helps your audience connect emotionally, creating a sense of relevance and urgency.

Minimizing Cognitive Load

Humans are wired to conserve mental energy, taking shortcuts whenever possible to avoid the cognitive load of System 2 thinking. Keep your slides, reports and presentations uncluttered and focused to accommodate this. Highlight only the essential data, stripping away anything extraneous that might divert attention or require unnecessary processing. When executives do not have to exert energy figuring out the meaning of the data, they are far more likely to make quick and confident decisions.

Ultimately, your role is to make financial information as 'brain-friendly' as possible. Present insights in an organized and visually appealing way that aligns with how the brain naturally processes information. Remember that your goal is to enable your executive audience to make the right decision quickly and confidently. Simplify the complex, use visuals to clarify and structure your narrative so that the flow of information makes sense intuitively. By respecting how your audience thinks you become an effective communicator, ensuring your insights are heard and acted upon.

A PICTURE IS WORTH A THOUSAND WORDS

The saying 'a picture is worth a thousand words' is especially true when presenting financial data. This idea is rooted in dual-coding (Paivio, 1991), which suggests that our brains process verbal and visual information through separate channels, making it easier to understand and retain a message when combined. By pairing visuals with words, whether in the form of speech or text, you activate these dual channels, enhancing the clarity and impact of your message (Figure 9.4).

Figure 9.4 Example of dual-coding.

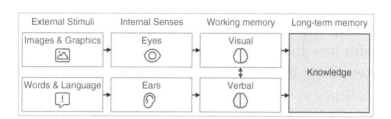

When an executive audience is presented with both a verbal explanation and a visual element, such as a chart or infographic, the two forms of information complement each other. This dual-coding process allows the audience to process and remember information more effectively. Visuals provide context, draw attention to key insights and allow for rapid pattern recognition, while the verbal component fills in details and adds explanatory depth.

Christian once had to present an initiative to improve the overall customer experience to the executive committee of a company running a chain of gyms. By implementing a new inventory management system the fitness equipment could be maintained and replaced more effectively, resulting in customers experiencing fewer equipment errors. Instead of presenting the elaborate data model behind the proposed investment, Christian accompanied his presentation with photos from the fitness centres, showcasing both broken and functioning equipment and the users' emotional state associated with both. By giving a verbal presentation while showing visuals related to the key messages, the recommendation was easy to decode, and management decided to move on to implementation.

The Split-Attention Effect

Interestingly, text and speech alone do not produce the same effect on the brain as combining visuals with verbal explanations. When presenting to an audience, lengthy written statements on slides can detract from the effectiveness of the verbal presentation. This is due to a cognitive effect known as the **split-attention effect** (Pouw et al., 2019), which occurs when your audience must divide their attention between reading the text on screen and listening to what you are saying.

The brain processes written and spoken words through the same verbal channel but cannot entirely focus on both simultaneously. When your audience reads detailed slides, they shift their attention away from your spoken message, as both activities require the same cognitive processing resources. This forces them to either read or listen, but not effectively do both simultaneously. As a result, comprehension and retention of both the visual text and the verbal message can be diminished.

This overload on the verbal processing channel decreases the audience's ability to follow along and increases cognitive strain, leading to poorer understanding and reduced engagement. To avoid this using brief bullet points, visuals or keywords that complement and enhance your spoken narrative is more effective. This allows the audience to simultaneously use both their visual and verbal cognitive channels without unnecessary competition. This approach helps maintain attention, enhances comprehension and improves the overall impact of your presentation.

PRE-ATTENTIVE ATTRIBUTES AND GESTALT PRINCIPLES

To enhance executives' quick and effective interpretation of financial data, you can leverage two powerful concepts from visual design: pre-attentive attributes and Gestalt principles. Both help simplify the decoding process, allowing your audience to grasp the key messages of your visuals effortlessly.

Pre-Attentive Attributes: Highlighting the Key Message Instantly

Pre-attentive attributes are visual elements the human brain processes almost instantaneously, even before conscious thought. These attributes include colour, size, shape, orientation and spatial positioning (Knaflic, 2015). By strategically using these elements in your charts and graphs, you can guide your audience's attention to the most critical parts of the data within milliseconds. For example, highlighting a key metric in a contrasting colour, increasing the size of a significant figure or using bold shapes for emphasis can help your audience immediately identify important patterns or outliers.

Consider the visuals in Figure 9.5 and reflect on how your attention is drawn to the odd ones in each. Before you are actively aware of it, your brain has spotted the element that does not fit the pattern.

Figure 9.5 Visual attention test example 1.

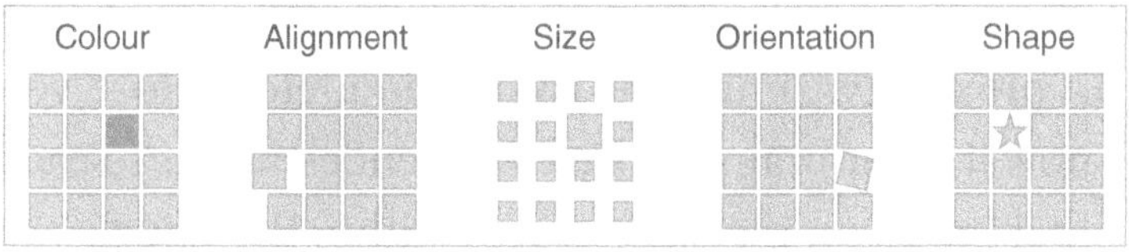

When used correctly, pre-attentive attributes make your visuals more intuitive. They allow executives to absorb the information quickly and reduce the cognitive effort required to understand your message.

Gestalt Principles: Organizing Information for Better Understanding

In addition to pre-attentive attributes, Gestalt principles guide how humans naturally perceive and organize visual elements. These principles, such as proximity, similarity, continuity and closure, can help you structure your visuals to align with how the brain processes information. For instance, grouping related data points (proximity) or using similar colours for similar categories (similarity) can help your audience understand relationships and hierarchies within your data more quickly. The principle of continuity allows you to create flow and connection across visuals, making it easier to follow trends over time.

Consider the visuals in Figure 9.6 and reflect on how your brain naturally groups the elements based on proximity, similarity, connection, etc. Before you know it, your brain has tied different elements to each other based on their placement within the visual.

Figure 9.6 Visual attention test example 2.

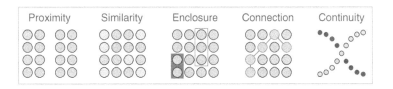

By applying Gestalt principles you can design visuals that look clean and professional and make the data easier to decode. This enables executives to comprehend the bigger picture and make informed decisions quickly.

Together, pre-attentive attributes and Gestalt principles are powerful tools for finance professionals to craft visuals that capture attention and clarify and simplify complex financial insights for faster decision-making.

TIPS FOR BETTER DATA VISUALIZATION

We could dedicate an entire book to data visualization practices, but a simple starting point that will get you far is to follow the following six guiding principles.

1. Pies Are for Eating – Not Presenting

Pie charts are often poor visualizations because they make it difficult for the audience to gauge volume accurately or compare the size of slices. Humans are not naturally adept at perceiving angles or areas. Unlike length, which our brains can assess more precisely, the volume represented by the slices of a pie chart can be challenging to interpret accurately, especially when differences between segments are subtle. This can lead to misunderstandings or underestimating the data's true proportions.

Bar charts, on the other hand, are much more effective because they represent data as lengths on a standard scale, allowing for quick and precise comparisons. The alignment of bars makes it easier for the eye to compare values, detect trends and identify significant differences, thus making bar charts a superior choice in most cases for conveying data clearly and accurately.

A key reason for the childhood game of drawing the shortest straw is that it is straightforward to gauge how the lengths of the straws compare. The sticks are like bars in a bar chart – easy to compare. This would be significantly more complicated if the game entailed comparing the volume of rocks, the size of leaves or any other alternative based on comparing volume or circumference.

Even marketing agencies leverage our inability to compare pies. This is why you often see pizza restaurants promoting two 12-inch pizzas as a better offer than one 18-inch pizza when you get less pizza by purchasing the two smaller ones. Doing the maths will show you that the size of an 18-inch pizza is greater than the sum of the two 12-inch pizzas. So, ditch the pie chart and find better alternatives that are easier to decode.

2. **Colours Are Not for Decoration**

When designing a data visual, colour is a powerful tool that can work for or against you. Used effectively, it can elegantly highlight key data points and signal change; when used poorly, it can create visual clutter and confuse your audience. As described in the section covering pre-attentive attributes your audience will pay attention to any colour that varies from the norm and try to assign meaning to that difference.

Consequently, the challenge is to use colour purposefully. Too many colours or contrasts can dilute your message and derail your audience's attention, while selective use of colours can guide your audience to the critical messages.

COMMUNICATING FINANCIALS TO EXECUTIVES

Thus, you should not use colours for decoration but to highlight critical messages or elements that need extraordinary attention. For example, it rarely makes sense to use different colours to distinguish different months or years from each other when visualizing a time series. On the other hand, it is usually prudent to use different colours for the different series, for example, a green line for our market share and a red line for the competitor's market share. So, use colours to highlight key points, not for decoration.

3. **Round as Much as You Can**
Reducing decimals is crucial when presenting financials to executives because it simplifies the message and focuses on the big picture. Management rarely needs the precision of the last cent to make strategic decisions, especially since there is always a degree of uncertainty involved in financial forecasting. Including fewer decimals or using units like mEUR (million euros) instead of EUR makes your charts and tables significantly easier to read and understand. This allows executives to quickly grasp the insights without getting bogged down in unnecessary detail, streamlining the decision-making process and enhancing the impact of your

Considerations on Data Visualizations

presentation. So, always round the values down as much as possible.

4. **Remove the Chart Junk**

Removing chart junk – unnecessary visual elements that do not contribute to understanding your data – is essential when presenting to executives. Every aspect of your chart should convey your key message clearly and efficiently. Elements like excess gridlines, redundant labels and decorative graphics often distract from the data, creating noise that obscures your insights.

By stripping away anything that does not add value you allow the core message to stand out, making it easier for executives to decode and interpret the information quickly. Even simplifying or removing elements like lines, axes or data labels can enhance clarity, allowing your audience to focus on the most essential points without unnecessary visual clutter. A clean, minimalist design directs attention where it matters and enables faster, more informed decision-making.

Less is more when it comes to data visualization. Just because you can make an elaborate graph does not mean you should. In most cases, you are better off stripping away complexity instead of adding it. You will not come off as brilliant by creating elaborate and complex charts – instead, you risk losing your audience and forgoing the opportunity to create impact. So, simplify relentlessly to present lean and clear visuals.

5. **Avoid Multidimensional Charts**
Using 3D or other multidimensional features in data visualizations can be detrimental when presenting to executives. The added depth distorts visual perception making it difficult to decode and compare values across multiple dimensions. In almost every case, adding a third dimension is unnecessary and does not contribute to a clearer understanding of the data.

If you need multiple dimensions to convey your message, it is likely a sign that the information may be too complex for a single visualization. Instead, break down the data into simpler visuals that allow the audience to process and interpret insights more quickly. Keeping your charts clean and two-dimensional ensures that the focus remains on the key takeaways, enabling management to quickly grasp the critical message without being overwhelmed by visual complexity.

So, refrain from using all the extra features available in Excel and PowerPoint. Adding 3D, shadows, reflections, etc., will not improve your presentation for your audience.

Considerations on Data Visualizations

6. Do not Present to Sherlock

Too often data visuals are presented without guidance on what to look for. Charts are presented without context, placing the executive audience in the role of Sherlock Holmes – the famous fictional detective – having to dissect the information and solve the mystery. This kind of hide-and-seek with insights often results in the audience reaching incorrect or at least alternative conclusions about the presented data. This can quickly derail your intended narrative as discussions about alternative interpretations disrupt the storyline.

Instead, you should highlight the main points in your data visualization to guide the audience's attention to the most relevant insights. Executives are often short on time and need to quickly understand the story the data are telling. Adding clear, concise text emphasizing key takeaways makes it easier for your audience to interpret the data accurately and focus on what matters most.

Always using action titles is a simple, often overlooked way to make decoding your data visualizations easier. In this context, an action title is a clear, descriptive headline for a data visualization that conveys the central insight or takeaway compellingly. Instead of merely stating what the data show (e.g., 'Sales by Region'), an action title emphasizes the conclusion or key message derived from the data (e.g., 'Northeast Region Drives 50% of Total Sales Growth'), helping the audience quickly understand the significance of the visual without having to interpret it themselves.

Furthermore, using labels, arrows or callouts to direct attention to important trends, outliers or significant shifts ensures that these critical data points are not overlooked. These visual cues enhance the clarity of your message and make the decision-making process more efficient by removing any ambiguity about what the data are meant to convey.

So, always add descriptive action headers and pinpoint the essential aspects of your data visualization using labels, callouts, arrows, etc.

TIPS FOR GREAT SLIDE MAKING

When presenting to executives you will often be backed by a slide deck. Here are a few tips to create a great slide deck that will support your presentation. See Figure 9.7 for an example.

Figure 9.7 Example of a perfect slide.

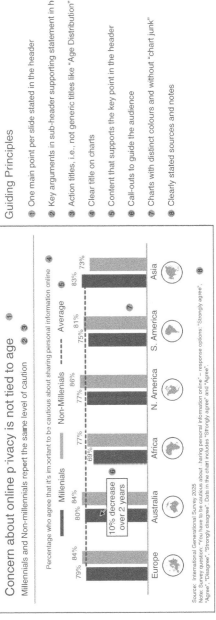

Place the Argument in the Header

Make your argument the slide's headline. This provides your audience with immediate insight into your main point. A strong argument-focused header, such as 'Cost Reduction Improves Profitability by 15%', keeps the slide focused and clear, guiding your audience directly to your point.

Use Action Titles in the Header and Charts

Write headers and chart titles that state the key action or insight directly, like 'Revenue Growth Driven by Product Innovation' or 'Market Share Increases in Key Regions'. These action-oriented titles act as mini-summaries, enabling the audience to instantly understand the takeaway from each visual element on the slide.

Stick to One Key Message per Slide

Structure each slide around a single, focused message. Ideally, the one stated in the header. This approach makes the presentation more digestible and reinforces your main points, ensuring that each slide communicates a clear takeaway without overwhelming the audience.

Present Only Evidence Supporting the Argument (in the Header) on the Slide

Include only data and visuals that directly support the argument in the header. Avoid extra details that can dilute your message. Keeping the slide streamlined ensures that the evidence is compelling. For instance, if your header says 'Customer Retention Boosts Profit', limit the content to metrics and visuals relevant to retention and profitability.

State Your Sources

Clearly display your data source in a small but visible font at the bottom of the slide or next to the charts. This establishes credibility and allows your audience to understand where the data originated, which builds trust in your analysis and conclusions.

Use Call-Outs to Highlight Key Points

Use call-out boxes or bold text to emphasize critical data points, like '+20% YoY' or 'Top 3 Cost-Reduction Levers'. Call-outs help the audience focus on the most crucial insights, making it easy to grasp the slide's main message without reading through all the details.

Use Colours to Make Charts Easy to Read

Choose a clear, consistent colour scheme with high-contrast colours to emphasize key segments, trends or growth areas. For instance, highlight positive trends in green and areas needing attention in red. Colour coding guides the audience's eye and enhances comprehension, making the visual data easy to interpret.

Use Large Readable Fonts

If presenting on a screen or projector, use large fonts that are readable from a distance. Legibility is essential, as it ensures everyone in the room can follow along, keeping your message accessible and clear to your audience. If the slides are intended for reading, smaller fonts can be applied.

CHAPTER TEN

HOW TO PREPARE THE PERFECT MANAGEMENT REPORT

We have now covered all five steps of communicating financials to executives and discussed some essential considerations for visual communication. It is time to put it all together in a mock-up management report. We aim to showcase what a near-perfect management report should look like. In principle, this should not vary by company or industry. However, you must adapt it to your target audience and the entity in focus.

When we insist on creating a management report in a specific way that differs from what the company

COMMUNICATING FINANCIALS TO EXECUTIVES

is already doing we often encounter varying objections. Here are a few examples.

- My stakeholders are detail-oriented, so I must show them the details upfront.
- It is vital to share all available information to cover my back and not make my stakeholders think I am hiding something from them.
- I want to ensure that all variances are visibly explained to showcase my knowledge of the numbers.
- Including everything I have uncovered in the management report helps my senior stakeholders see how hard I have worked to create the report and will reward me for my hard work.

We have already dispelled most of these objections in previous chapters. However, if we boil it down to one objection buster, it is lack of trust. If you need to use any of these objections your stakeholders do not trust you. In the ideal world, they trust your analysis and chosen method to present the management report, meaning you can adapt the structure we have presented in the five steps and lead them through your storyline.

We recognize that trust needs to be built, and for various reasons, you may need to take some sidesteps before you can jump straight into presenting the perfect management report. This could be because the finance function is not trusted or because you are new in the role.

In this case, you must also lower your ambitions for the first couple of presentation rounds. You may use the first meeting only to present the financial status and gain confidence from your target audience that you know the details. In the next meeting you may present the key attention points and have the financial status ready if needed. Finally, in the third meeting you can present ideas to address the critical attention points. In this way, you can build trust in your management reporting in a structured manner within just a few meetings.

An old saying from Dutch politician Johan Thorbecke in 1848 goes like this: 'Trust arrives on foot but leaves on horseback'. That means you cannot disregard the rigor that should go into preparing the management report at any time. If management spots errors, it will erode their trust and confidence in you.

STRUCTURING YOUR MANAGEMENT REPORT

We have now agreed as a rule that you should use the structure presented in this book except when you are experiencing significant trust issues. We can then proceed to present a structure for your management report. We have seen significant variance regarding the length of management reports. We would not recommend that it be longer than ten pages. We have even seen an example of an excellent management report on two pages only. This included the financial status and key attention points to facilitate the management discussion. Here is what your management report structure could look like:

- **Page 1:** The front page has a nice visual that also details the entity in scope, the period covered, the audience it is prepared for, who prepared it and the date of report preparation.
- **Page 2:** The entity's financial status in the given period is covered, with comments and colour coding of the critical variances for easy identification.
- **Page 3:** The key attention points you suggest being discussed in the meeting or that you will address on the next page.
- **Page 4:** The main recommendations or critical insights to address the key attention points.
- **Page 5:** The significant arguments for following your recommendations.
- **Page 6:** The overall risks and assumptions involved in moving forward and the expected benefits from implementing your recommendations.

- **Page 7:** A high-level implementation plan for your recommendations.
- **Page 8:** A summary slide highlighting the decisions to be made to ensure this is confirmed before ending the meeting and what would be the next steps.
- **Appendix 1:** A detailed income statement, balance sheet and cash flow with variance explanations of all variances above an agreed threshold.
- **Appendix 2:** A revenue and cost breakdown into your dominant dimensions, i.e. customer, product, geography, etc., and a line-by-line cost review.
- **Appendix 3:** Relevant facts uncovered during your analysis that support your recommendation.

This is essentially what you need in a perfect management report. Depending on the complexity and potential impact of the key attention points and recommended solutions, pages 3 and 4 may extend to a few more pages. Also, depending on the meeting type, you may dedicate a page to show the most recent forecast, underlining what will happen if management does nothing to address the key attention points.

It is important to remember that you may not need to go through everything, even in this condensed management report. If you gain buy-in and acceptance of a recommendation early on from your audience you can move swiftly to the implementation plan and confirm the next steps. Conversely, you may be stopped early in your presentation during the financial status, needing to detail further specific variances. You can quickly jump to the relevant appendix and highlight your knowledge of the situation.

A MOCK-UP OF THE PERFECT MANAGEMENT REPORT

Let us return to Sarah and her journey with management reporting and her challenges communicating financials to executives. This section will show a more comprehensive example of a management report. This is not necessarily aligned with where Sarah landed with her presentation in our previous chapters. However, we think it is important to show the full breadth of what a management report should include, tackling the issues of all relevant stakeholders.

Sarah had spent considerable time getting to know her stakeholders and can summarize their main issues as follows:

- **Chief Commercial Officer:** An unproductive sales force and a weak logic between the sales pipeline and the business they would win.

- **Chief Operations Officer:** Poor on-time delivery and poor accurate delivery of exactly what Sales had sold.
- **Chief People Officer:** Challenges in producing accurate FTE numbers and other undefined value-adding challenges to be solved later.

Sarah must showcase her understanding of their issues and her analysis of the situation in the management report. We will start by showcasing page 2, Solara Tech's financial status (Figure 10.1).

We should note that because the book is in black only, we have not applied a colour scheme to the visuals. Instead of using arrows, you could colour the boxes to highlight variances from the budget and apply the same colour scheme to the comment boxes.

Figure 10.1 Page 2 of the management report.

Poor sales and operational delivery issues cut operating income in half.

Profit & Loss Statement

mUSD	Actual '24	Budget '24	Forecast '25	
Revenue	↓ 75	80	85	Poor revenue performance was driven by poor sales productivity and weak pipeline.
Cost of goods sold	↑ 50	48	55	Higher than expected costs due to on-time delivery struggles.
Gross profit	↓ 25	32	30	
Operating expenses	↑ 18	15	20	Operating expenses are negatively impacted by consultant spending to deliver new solutions as sold by sales.
Operating income	↓ 7	17	10	Operating income is less than half the budget and isn't expected to improve significantly. Hence, we should discuss an action plan.

She uses the header to outline the main issues and sticks to a few key accounts in her summary. All comments highlight the why instead of pinpointing what is happening in the period.

You will notice how Sarah sticks to the facts on the financial status. She repeats the comments made by the management team members, which should remove any complications in presenting the financial status. This sets Sarah up to highlight the key attention points on page 3 of her report (Figure 10.2).

Sarah showcases the main issues the management team members have highlighted and comments on these developments based on her analysis of the numbers and discussions with team members in the

Figure 10.2 Page 3 of the management report.

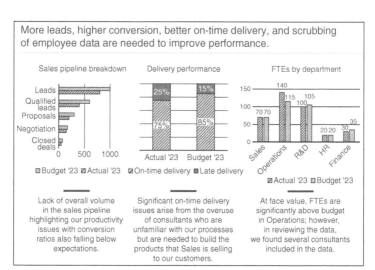

different departments. As such, these should not be controversial. However, they may cause friction between the management team members, i.e. the CCO and COO, when the COO highlights Sales as the main reason for having so many consultants. Also, the Chief People Officer may point to the COO as the cause of the poor FTE data.

Therefore, the key attention points slides should allow discussion and alignment on the issues. Sarah should also facilitate prioritization of which issues cause the most significant performance challenges. She should challenge the management team members and seek to mediate if they get into a heated argument. Once an alignment has been reached on the key attention points, Sarah can turn her attention to the recommended actions to address them on page 4 of her report (Figure 10.3).

Sarah recommends plenty of actions to address the performance issues. However, she is also leaning towards prioritizing what to do first. This can be challenging to prepare in advance since the management team may align on other issues on the previous page; however, in this case, we are still prepared to discuss which actions are most appropriate.

Sarah does not currently need the exact solution ready for management. No one likes to be told what to do so they must have an opportunity to direct the solutions and get their team(s) involved in designing

COMMUNICATING FINANCIALS TO EXECUTIVES

Figure 10.3 Page 4 of the management report.

Let's prioritize on-time delivery first, as we shouldn't scale our revenue without a strong delivery process.

Sales Pipeline	• Implement targeted sales training to improve conversion rates. • Develop a more robust pipeline tracking system that aligns sales efforts with realistic outcomes. • Consider revising sales incentives to align with profitable deals rather than just volume.
On-Time Delivery	• Improve communication and collaboration between Sales and Operations to ensure that sales commitments align with operational capabilities. • Invest in process improvements that can streamline production and supply chain management. • Consider implementing a sales and operations planning (S&OP) process to align sales forecasts with production schedules better.
FTE Data	• Implement a more robust HR system to track employee data accurately and in real-time. • Develop workforce planning strategies to ensure the company has the right number of employees with the right skills in the right places. • Address employee engagement and retention strategies to reduce turnover and improve productivity.

the final solution. If Sarah did not have this page and came up with no recommended actions, she could not steer the discussion and risk becoming irrelevant for the remainder of the meeting.

When presenting a recommendation based on the different options, it is vital that Sarah also presents the main arguments. This is needed to build confidence in the recommended actions and allows management to challenge the recommendation and potentially suggest a different option. Page 5 of the management report contains the most significant arguments for the recommendation (Figure 10.4).

Figure 10.4   Page 5 of the management report.

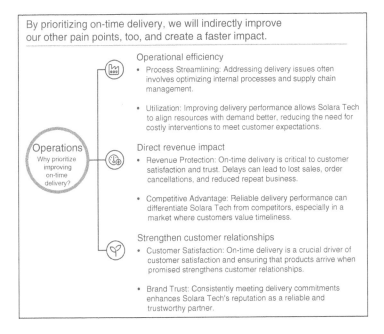

You will notice how Sarah addresses the operational concerns and the potential commercial impact, which should help align the management team with this recommendation. Had she only focused on the operational benefits, she would likely have difficulty convincing the CCO to prioritize fixing on-time delivery.

It is not vital that management agrees with Sarah's recommendation or a comes up with a different one. What is essential is that Sarah has provided relevant insights and suggested actions to improve performance in her communication with management.

COMMUNICATING FINANCIALS TO EXECUTIVES

For the next few pages in the management report, we will proceed as if they agreed to her recommendation of improving on-time delivery first. Page 6 of the management report contains key risks, assumptions and expected benefits (Figure 10.5).

Page 6 of the report is not meant as a detailed walkthrough; potentially, the text can be slimmed to just the bold headings. However, we wanted to illustrate the depth of the analysis needed to make this recommendation. Sarah must show that she has

Figure 10.5   Page 6 of the management report.

The benefits of addressing these issues are significant as they are expected to bring operating expenses back in line with the budget.

Assumptions	Risks	Expected benefits
• Stable Demand: The plan assumes that customer demand will remain stable or grow in line with forecasts.	• Supply Chain Disruptions: Improvements in on-time delivery may be challenged by disruptions in the supply chain.	• Increased Customer Satisfaction and Retention: Improving on-time delivery enhances the company's reliability, building customer trust.
• Supplier Reliability: The strategy assumes that suppliers will maintain or improve their performance in delivering inputs on time and of the expected quality.	• Resource Allocation: Prioritizing on-time delivery improvements might require reallocating resources from other areas, such as R&D or marketing.	• Revenue Growth: Satisfied customers are more likely to place repeat orders, which can drive consistent revenue growth. Improved delivery performance can be a selling point for attracting new clients.
• Internal Capacity: The plan assumes that Solara Tech has or can develop the internal capacity to implement the necessary changes.	• Increased Costs: Enhancing delivery performance may involve additional costs.	
• Customer Tolerance: It is assumed that customers will tolerate any temporary disruptions or delays that may occur during the implementation of process improvements.	• Employee Resistance: Changes in processes or expectations may face resistance from employees, particularly if they require new workflows, training or shifts in responsibilities.	• Cost Savings: The company can lower transportation costs by improving process efficiency and reducing the need for last-minute, expedited shipping options.
		• Operational Efficiency: Focusing on improving delivery performance often leads to more streamlined and efficient processes, which can reduce waste and improve overall productivity.

considered multiple options on the previous slide and has done detailed work on the recommended actions. Usually, you would also aim to specify the specific financial benefits expected from this recommendation and some KPIs you would use to track its impact.

In principle, mitigating actions could also be discussed here. However, they are best considered when working on detailed solutions, at which time a more thorough action plan can be presented.

This page adds much credibility to the proposed actions. However, in this case, these must be prepared in collaboration with the operations department as otherwise there will likely be more resistance to the recommendations and the analysis behind them. Ideally, this page builds momentum for the recommendation and allows you to move to the implementation plan. In Sarah's case, she does not have a final solution yet, but it still makes sense to show a high-level implementation plan or, in some cases, at a minimum, the following steps. Page 7 of the management report shows a high-level implementation plan (Figure 10.6).

As Sarah does not have a specific solution yet, she highlights the more generic project phases she is proposing to get a team together and to work on the project. She should expect challenges from management regarding the plan because it shows they are invested in finding a solution and want to ensure it works. Here

Figure 10.6   Page 7 of the management report.

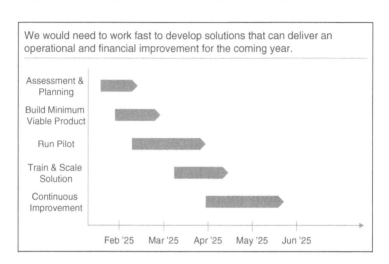

she should also ask which team members from their teams should be a part of the project. In this case it should involve Sales and Operations resources, as a lack of coordination is part of the root cause of Solara Tech's performance issue.

We are getting to the end of Sarah's management presentation with only the summary slide left to present. You can see how the presentation enabled Sarah to control and facilitate the meeting. The aim is not necessarily to get a quick 'Yes' to go and work on the challenges. While getting a 'Yes' and alignment on the key challenges is essential, getting constructive feedback from management on the suggested actions is just as important. It will likely not deliver progress if they do not stand behind it. In the summary slide we

How to Prepare the Perfect Report

get the final buy-in and acceptance to take the next steps. Too often we leave meetings without a clear plan or agreed actions. Sarah needs to ensure this is not the case for Solara Tech. Figure 10.7 shows page 8 of the management report summarizing the meeting and the next steps.

Ending the meeting like this ensures that decisions are made, that the next steps are agreed upon, and that Sarah is mandated to start executing the decisions. It is clear to management what needs to

Figure 10.7 Page 8 of the management report.

We should act on on-time delivery to improve performance in the first half of the coming year.	
Key takeaway	• Sales Pipeline Issues: Addressed the disconnect between the sales pipeline and actual business wins, emphasizing the need for improved sales productivity. • On-Time Delivery: Identified delivery delays as a critical issue impacting customer satisfaction and revenue. • Workforce Management: Discussed the need for better employee tracking and alignment with operational needs.
Agreed actions	• Management team to move forward with the 6-month plan focusing on rapid assessment, process optimization, and technology integration. • Confirm assignment of project leads and teams responsible for each phase of the implementation plan. • Identify a project manager to oversee the entire process and ensure alignment with strategic goals.
Next steps	• Immediate Start: Begin the assessment and planning phase immediately in January 2025. Schedule the first progress meeting for mid-January to review initial findings. • Commitment to Execution: Confirm commitment from all management team members to support the project and ensure its success.

happen, and they feel confident in Sarah's ability to deliver.

We will not cover the appendices in this book as we know you know how to prepare these and what to include. This report likely looks quite different from any report you have ever seen or submitted yourself. You may doubt whether it will be effective and even be accepted by your management team. As mentioned earlier, we recognize that you may have situation where you need to start in a different place to establish trust and credibility in your work. However, we highly encourage you to strive to reshape your management report to fit the format and structure that we have presented here. We guarantee it will lead to better management meetings, decision-making and performance. In the next chapter, we will cover alternative uses of the five-step communication model presented in this book, which will be useful to finance professionals.

CHAPTER ELEVEN

HOW FINANCE PROFESSIONALS BECOME EXCELLENT COMMUNICATORS

We have covered how finance professionals can communicate financials to executives and showed a specific example of how the perfect management report could look. However, the principles for communication that we have laid out have many more uses for finance professionals to achieve excellence in all their communication.

The management report is likely the most structured communication we frequently share. However,

COMMUNICATING FINANCIALS TO EXECUTIVES

we also prepare and present business cases, conduct ad hoc analyses and communicate extensively inside and outside the Finance department. Most of this communication is inefficient, and while this is not unique to finance professionals, our technical nature usually magnifies the issue. That is why it will benefit us to expand our newfound way of communicating financials to executives in other areas.

To do this we should start with the SCQA framework, the most fundamental principle behind the five-step communication principles.

- **Situation:** The widely accepted facts about the current situation that we can all agree on.
- **Complication:** The problem or opportunity that we must address to change the current situation. If we do not address it, the current situation will become worse, or we will lose the opportunity.
- **Question:** The key question we should explore to solve the complication. This question should usually be formulated in a way that makes it unambiguous. We can leverage the SMART principle (Doran, 1981).
- **Answer:** The solution to the question or recommendation we put forward for management to consider. This may present with multiple options when solving more complex complications.

218

Let us look at two simple examples:

Example 1: The Chinese competitor

- **Situation:** Sales are down 4%.
- **Complication:** A new Chinese competitor has entered the market.
- **Question:** How can we regain the lost sales before the end of the year?
- **Answer:** Re-position our product into the premium product segment.

Example 2: The production defects

- **Situation:** The number of defects in production is up by 10%.
- **Complication:** The turnover among production employees has doubled in the past 24 months.
- **Question:** How can we increase production quality to the 99% target?
- **Answer:** We should introduce quality assurance and a retention program for employees.

Both examples could quickly summarize the monthly management report, backed by further analysis. They could also summarize an ad hoc analysis. This approach is also usually used in problem-solving, where the gap between the question and answer is covered in the problem-solving process. It works for written and verbal communication and in almost all situations. When communicating about challenging situations, e.g. company layoffs, you would share more details and analysis before stating the answer.

Imagine that you instituted a general rule in your finance function that all communication, including e-mails, had to follow this principle. That would make a massive difference. To exemplify this further, we can go back to the example of the Chinese competitor. Here, Anders sent two different e-mails (Figures 11.1 and 11.2) about the situation to his managing partner, Michael.

WITHOUT USING SCQA

Figure 11.1   Email without using SQCA.

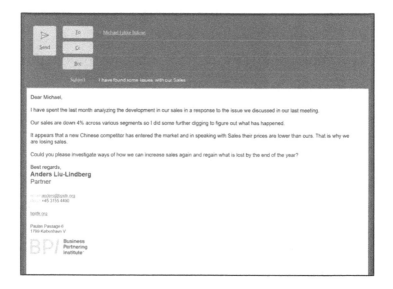

Figure 11.2 Email using SQCA.

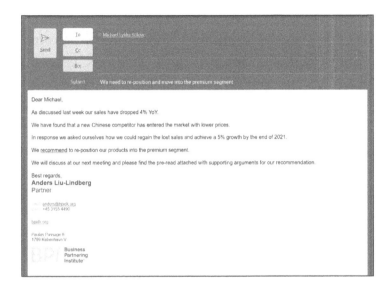

WITH THE USE OF SCQA

You may think the e-mails are similar; however, you will notice that the first e-mail includes no recommendation but imposes the problem on Michael to figure out. In the second e-mail, the recommendation is clearly outlined and ready to be discussed in an upcoming meeting. Undoubtedly, the second e-mail has a much higher chance of moving towards solving the complication.

COMMUNICATING FINANCIALS TO EXECUTIVES

BUSINESS CASES

Another typical communication finance professionals make is submitting a business case for approval. Like the simple e-mail, the SCQA principle should be used to communicate the recommendation that management should approve. You will also need to underline your main arguments for the recommendation and have the supporting facts ready in an appendix should you be challenged with your recommendation.

In addition, we need to extend the communication with a few additional elements.

- **Benefit case:** You would usually include in the recommendation a high-level statement about the benefits of implementing your solution. However, this needs to be explicitly underlined in your communication to showcase how you have derived the benefits and why you think they can be realized. There should be a monetary effect put forward. Even if the immediate benefits are soft, these should be recalculated to hard benefits, e.g. hours saved recalculated into money saved.
- **Risks and assumptions:** When solving any problem and making a recommendation, we usually make assumptions about what must be

true for the solution to be a good solution. These assumptions need to be documented and communicated. Similarly, any decision carries risks that should be highlighted alongside potential mitigating actions.

- **Implementation plan:** Beyond the immediate next steps, which should always be clear, you must present a more elaborate implementation plan when presenting a business case. This should include significant milestones, resources needed, who should be involved, etc. This will make it easier for management to say yes as they know what will happen next and what is needed from them.

When you combine all this, you have the full Pyramid Principle in use, and have built a logical and compelling communication for your recommendation.

FROM ANALYSIS TO PRESENTATION

Completing the analysis is one thing, but as discussed, putting it into a presentation is another. The good thing is that you can easily translate this into a presentation by using the Pyramid Principle. Below, we showcase how each element in the pyramid – SCQA, arguments, facts and the additional elements – becomes a specific section in your business case presentation (Figure 11.3).

As a logical consequence, this also means that you must present your recommendation within the first three slides. This should be done within five minutes, meaning you will catch the attention of the audience, assuming you are working on a priority that interests them.

Now, you can start to build your presentation. However, do not open your presentation tool just yet. Instead, find a whiteboard or a simple piece of paper and start drawing a storyboard. For the storyboard, you should follow these simple principles.

- There should only be one key message on each slide.
- Find key visuals and facts to support your message.
- Tell a coherent and compelling story.

The key message should be placed as the slide's header rather than a generic header. Here are two examples using the example of a Chinese competitor.

- **Generic:** Overview of sales development in the period.
- **Storyline:** Sales are down 4% due to the entry of a new Chinese competitor.

Figure 11.3 From pyramid to presentation mode.

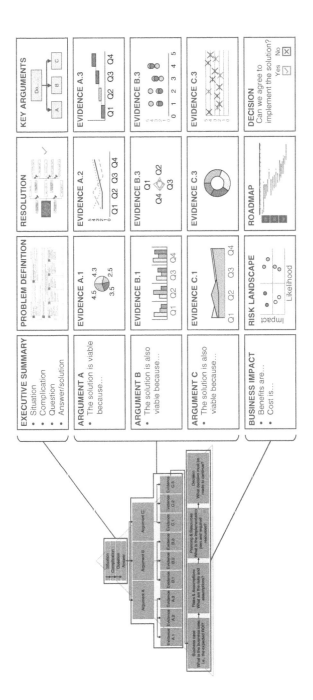

You immediately catch the conclusion and key message of the slide with a storyline heading, whereas with a generic heading, you would have to look for the answer somewhere on the slide. It may even be hidden in a large text block or among several highlighted callouts. To check your storytelling, copy and paste all your headings into a separate document and read it aloud. It should then be obvious where you need to make changes to make the story more coherent and compelling. Essentially, you want to reach a point where the reader or audience, by flipping through the slides, can easily understand what you are trying to communicate by reading the headings only.

ONE SIZE DOES NOT FIT ALL

While the overall principles of communication outlined here can be used for almost any form of communication, this does not mean you should not adjust your communication to your audience – the type of audience and style of presentation matter to how you communicate your messages. Let us review some examples.

- **Presentation:** This could be a town hall meeting or conference presentation. Here, you will tell your story in your own words and use very visual slides to support your key messages. Do not use your slides as speaker notes because it will automatically turn your attention away from the audience.

- **Management meeting:** This is usually a presentation or discussion with a team in a meeting setting. Here, you will simplify your presentation to key facts and supporting arguments. As we have outlined in this book, you want to structure your presentation to drive decision-making. Do not repeat slides and material you have already shared in a pre-read, or things that the audience is assumed to know already.
- **Reporting:** This is written communication where you do not get to present your messages in person. You want to use a clear and intuitive structure, starting with the answer using the SCQA principle. Your communication should be self-explanatory, as you cannot add context or explain any inconsistencies. Do not include details that do not support your key message, which would confuse the reader.

We know this will add even more work to your communication efforts but will significantly increase your impact.

COMMUNICATING FINANCIALS TO EXECUTIVES

FINAL TIPS ON COMMUNICATION

You have finally done it! Your presentation is ready, and you have followed all the principles outlined here and are prepared to present. However, you may want to consider these final communication tips to increase your impact further.

Before the meeting

- Make sure you rehearse the presentation when it is a crucial presentation. As most finance professionals are not natural presenters, we need to try to look the part in front of an audience. You can do this alone in front of the mirror or ask a colleague or manager to act as the audience and give you feedback.
- Show up early for the presentation even if the venue is unavailable before the meeting starts. Nothing is worse for an audience than a presenter who is late or spends the first five minutes of the meeting getting ready.
- Check the technology upfront to ensure you do not run into challenges with equipment, e.g. the cable does not fit your laptop, since this could

all be avoided if you checked in with the venue beforehand.

- Relax! You have put in all the work, and it looks great. No one knows more about this topic than you do, and you have all the detailed arguments and facts ready if needed. There is no reason to be nervous. You have got this!

At the meeting

- Start strongly using a good hook. The SCQA principle works nicely here, so most work is done upfront.
- Be concise since less is more. This may sound like a cheeky marketing statement but consider your audience's perspective. They are busy with little time, and getting into too many details does not help anyone.
- Agree upfront on the purpose of the meeting. This will save many explanations and allow the audience to object to or modify the purpose in case they see it differently.
- Steer the meeting to help reach a conclusion. Remember that you run the meeting – not the audience. This does not mean you should discourage discussion and thoughtful disagreements; it simply means you have the right to

move things along if a discussion gets stuck, for instance, by putting items on the 'parking lot.'

- Appreciate challenges from the audience, as they show interest in your presentation and recommendation. Do not get into a fight with them but try to explore things from their perspective and make sure their views become part of the solution if they are relevant.

After the meeting

- Document decisions and next steps and share a summary via e-mail to offer your audience a final opportunity to add context or objections.
- Finally, ask the audience or individual participants for feedback. This is the best way to improve before the next time.

These are all relevant points to consider, especially for important presentations. Anders recalls one presentation he did once where the preparation was stellar, and everything started well. However, when it came to audience members asking questions, he quickly got defensive about the solution and appeared unwilling to listen. In receiving feedback afterward, this dragged down the overall impression of Anders as a presenter and had a negative impact early on in his career. This shows that it is possible to fail at any step and that a good analysis is far from the entire effort.

You should now have a good understanding of additional uses of the principles for communicating financials to executives. Undoubtedly, they can transform your career and your impact as a presenter. However, they also require time and effort to learn and implement into your communications. We will dedicate the book's final chapter to how to do this.

CHAPTER TWELVE

PRACTICAL STEPS TO START IMPROVING YOUR COMMUNICATION SKILLS

Theory is one thing but it is quite another to do things in real life, on the job and under the pressure of presenting to senior executives. Most finance professionals have much to improve before they can nail their executive communication of financials to non-financial professionals. In this book we have laid out a path for you to start the journey, not least by sharing our five-step framework for financial communication.

As you read this final chapter, you have likely started thinking about how to implement each of the steps and other tips we shared. That is if you are not like Sarah and have practiced each step along with reading each chapter. We know how hard it is to start working in new ways. We train hundreds of finance professionals annually in executive communication and other topics that are usually outside their comfort zone. That is also why our learning journeys typically extend across six or more months. This allows the learners enough time to digest the contents of each learning module and try their learnings on the job.

Like most others in learning and development, we believe in the 70/20/10 approach to learning: 70% of learning is on-the-job training, 20% is sparring with leaders, colleagues and other role models, and only 10% is formal training sessions. You can consider this book a training session, meaning you still have 90% of your learning to cover if you want to become an expert communicator of financials.

In this chapter, we aim to share some practical approaches you can apply to start tackling the 90% and leave you with concrete steps to try immediately. We can say that if you do not take any action to apply the learnings from this book during the next monthly cycle you will likely not start applying any of the concepts at all. So, let us make sure that you get started together!

Practical Steps to Improving Communication Skills

TAKING THE FIRST STEPS

It is all about taking the first steps, and, to help you, we wanted to share some practical steps you can take without too much effort. In chronological order these are:

- Compare your current management report with the five-step framework.
- Ask your colleagues/team members for feedback.
- Ask your audience for feedback.
- Prepare a mock-up and ask for more feedback.
- Launch and drive continuous improvement.

Comparison and Feedback

The most straightforward first step is to look at your current management report. How does it stack up against the five-step framework? You can conduct your self-assessment but do not leave it at that. Ask your colleagues or team members for feedback too. We encourage you to schedule a small session with them to debrief on what you have learned about the five-step framework. Teaching others is one of the best ways to learn new things yourself because it forces you to think through the concepts and how to explain them to others.

Ask Your Audience

Once you have completed the self-assessment, including talking with other finance professionals, you should interview the senior stakeholders who receive the management report. What is their impression of the management report, how does it help them take action and what improvement suggestions would they have? It is unlikely that their feedback will align perfectly with the five-step framework, but you must show in the new management report that you take their feedback seriously. It is visible in the changes you have made.

Prepare Your Mock-Up

Now that you have collected all the feedback you need, it is time to start preparing the new management report. Ideally, you do this with old data, i.e. the previous monthly management report, but feel free to use any relevant dataset. Ensure you complete the report in full and get another round of feedback. This will prepare you to put the new management report into production.

Practical Steps to Improving Communication Skills

This is a similar approach to the one Anders undertook when he started to support a VP and his team of product managers. We shared this story earlier relating to a P&L review; however, Anders also applied a similar approach when starting a new financial performance review cycle with each product manager. It did not exactly follow the five-step approach but Anders applied a different approach in utilizing the strategy material each product manager had created for their product. This included initiatives and targets of what to achieve. Anders then used it to make a performance review package, which he ran his stakeholders through monthly. One of their first comments was, 'I did not even know Finance could do that'. We are not making guarantees here, but we are confident you will receive similar comments as you embark on this journey.

Implement and Continuous Improvement

You should not expect that you can create a standard package and then populate it with new numbers every month. No, it is a living document that, every month, needs to cater to changing priorities and new opportunities and risks. You should treat the monthly process (or whichever cycle is relevant for your performance reviews) as a continuous improvement cycle. We know this requires much work; hence it is essential that you set up a proper and efficient data flow, which we discussed when we unfolded step #1 in the framework. Otherwise you will always run out of time, and your reviews of performance will end up incomplete and lacking in impact.

THE NEXT STEPS

Getting this new cycle up and running in a steady state will likely take months, and you will also need to prove its benefits in the form of improved performance and customer satisfaction. Now comes the hard part. Convincing others that it is a good idea, not least those outside your immediate team whom you have included as part of your journey. They have not read the book and have not sat in your management meetings and experienced the transformation that you have. That is why you need to show that you are a skilled communicator of financials and master change management. Here, it is also helpful to utilize a proven framework. We recommend using ADKAR (Hiatt, 2006):

- Awareness.
- Desire.
- Knowledge.
- Ability.
- Reinforcement.

Awareness

We have discussed why finance professionals must change how they communicate financials to executives, especially those outside finance. We recommend using similar arguments with other finance professionals in your finance function or broader network. Without awareness, they will not understand the need for change and will be content with continuing their current ways of working.

Desire

You can share your story and the impact equation to ignite their desire to change their working methods. Empathize with them on their potential lack of impact due to low influence, which can be significantly improved by improving their communication skills. If there is no desire to change, they may understand your logical reasoning, but they will not make the new ways of working a part of their working lives.

Knowledge

Now, your target group is ready for some more formal training. You may not be able to train them yourself beyond showing them what you have done, so you may need to enlist support from HR or the Learning and Development team. You should also feel free to reach out to us directly. It cannot be understated how important this step is, even if it is 'only' 10% of the learning effort.

Ability

We have all been to a training program, which was nice but did not lead to any change once we returned to our daily routines. Here, you play an essential role for your colleagues as a sparring partner and role model. Offer your support to help them go through the steps you have gone through, as we outlined earlier in this chapter. It is critical that they too take the first steps soon after they have received the formal training. Alternatively, you can give them this book to help them gain more knowledge and ability.

Reinforcement

As mentioned, it takes some months to establish the new working methods. To help your colleagues through this crucial period, you could form a community of finance professionals who have all gained the knowledge and ability to become excellent financial communicators. Host frequent community meetings where you share success stories from past presentations, feedback from business leaders and concrete examples of how it has improved performance. It will also allow members to share what they find challenging or ask questions about how to succeed. Other ways exist to reinforce the new behaviors, but establishing a community typically works well within a company.

FROM STEPS TO A NEW COMPANY CULTURE

Imagine yourself a few years after you finish reading this book. You have followed all the steps in the book first to become a skilled financial communicator yourself, then trained others and finally made it an ingrained part of recruitment and onboarding to hire and train skilled financial communicators. Now, your company culture is changing and everyone is working differently. Business leaders get focused insights from the finance function, significantly aiding their decision-making. Better decisions are made as a result, and because the financial performance review cycle tracks the impact of the decisions and actions that follow closely it will ultimately lead to better business results.

It may seem far-fetched that reading one book can lead to your company gaining a competitive advantage. This is not achieved overnight but requires years of consistent effort to change how the company works. It is possible to make it happen and we are certainly rooting for you!

It should go without saying that finance professionals need to improve their communication of financials. Almost everything we do boils down to this moment and today we often fall short. This severely limits our impact and has business leaders thinking their finance function is not adding much value to the company and should merely be considered a cost centre.

To realize our potential as advisors we should start to communicate differently. In this book, we have shared a concrete five-step framework, which is built on the Pyramid Principle by Barbara Minto. This is a proven framework for communication that consultants across the globe use, and now it is time for you to start using it too. We have adapted it to financial communication, and ironically, if you start to use it and learn to master it you will soon be using it to beat the consultants at their work. Never again shall management bring in external consultants to do your work because you failed to communicate your insights in a way they understand.

You have an advantage by having access to key decision-making, financial and non-financial data, an overview of the company's value chain, analytical skills and business acumen. The ability to communicate financials to executives is the final piece of the puzzle. No consultant can beat you to it and business leaders will love you for it. It will be to the extent that they will never make any critical decisions again without consulting with you first.

IT IS TIME TO GET TO WORK

We hope you are as excited as we are about improving your financial communication skills. It can significantly transform your career and help you reach all the goals you have set for yourself. We highly encourage you to share your journey with the world, e.g. on LinkedIn, at conferences and with your network. You can also share your journey directly with us. Contact them on LinkedIn to discuss your journey and get more tips about improving your financial communication skills and other skills that will help you increase your influence.

It is time to put down the book and get to work. All good intentions matter nothing if action is not taken. In this final chapter, we have outlined the practical steps for you to take to start your journey. All you need to do is take the first step...

REFERENCES

Doran, George (1981). There's a S.M.A.R.T. way to write management's goals and objectives. AMA Forum. https://community.mis.temple.edu/mis0855002fall2015/files/2015/10/S.M.A.R.T-Way-Management-Review.pdf. Accessed 30 November 2024.

Dunn, Matthew (2023). Is a picture worth a 1,000 words or 60,000 words in marketing? Email Audience. https://www.emailaudience.com/research-picture-worth-1000-words-marketing. Accessed 30 November 2024.

Dykes, Brent (2020). *Effective Data Storytelling*. Wiley.

Farrell, Marcy (2023). Data and Intuition: Good Decisions Need Both. Harvard Business Publishing: Corporate Learning. https://www.harvardbusiness.org/data-and-intuition-good-decisions-need-both. Accessed 30 November 2024.

Hiatt, Jeff (2006). *ADKAR: A Model for Change in Business, Government and our Community*. Prosci Learning Center Publications.

REFERENCES

Kahneman, Daniel (2011). *Thinking, Fast and Slow*. Farrar, Straus and Giroux.

Kang, Weixi, Guzman, Kreisha Lou and Malvaso, Antonio (2023). Big Five personality traits in the workplace: Investigating personality differences between employees, supervisors, managers, and entrepreneurs. *Frontiers in Psychology*. https://www.frontiersin.org/journals/psychology/articles/10.3389/fpsyg.2023.976022/full. Accessed 30 November 2024.

Knaflic, Cole Nussbaumer (2015). *Storytelling With Data: A Data Visualization Guide for Business Professionals*. Wiley.

Lafley, A. G. and Martin, Roger (2013). *Playing to Win*. Harvard Business Review Press.

Maister, David, Green, Charles and Galford, Robert (2001). *The Trusted Advisor*. Simon & Schuster.

Mark, Gloria (2023). Speaking of Psychology: Why our attention spans are shrinking, with Gloria Mark, PhD. American Psychological Association. https://www.apa.org/news/podcasts/speaking-of-psychology/attention-spans. Accessed 30 November 2024.

McSpadden, Kevin (2015). You Now Have a Shorter Attention Span Than a Goldfish. Time. https://time.com/3858309/attention-spans-goldfish. Accessed 30 November 2024.

Miller, George A. (1994). The Magical Number Seven, Plus or Minus Two: Some Limits on Our Capacity for Processing Information. *Psychological Review* 101(2): 343–52.

Minto, Barbara (2010). *The Pyramid Principle*. Prentice Hall.

Noto, Grace (2022). *CFOs log shortest tenure in C-suite: study*. CFO Dive. https://www.cfodive.com/news/cfos-log-shorter-tenures-higher-pay-demand-spikes-study-datarails/639240. Accessed 30 November 2024.

Paivio, Allan (1991). Dual Coding Theory: Retrospect And Current Status. *Canadian Journal of Psychology/ Revue Canadienne de Psychologie*, 45(3): 255–287.

Pouw, Wim, Rop, Gertjan, de Koning, Bjorn and Paas, Fred (2019). The cognitive basis for the split-attention effect. *Journal of Experimental Psychology: General*, 148(11): 2058–2075.

Rock, David and Ringleb, Al (2013). *Handbook of NeuroLeadership*. CreateSpace Independent Publishing Platform.

Rudder, Alana, Main, Kelly and Watts, Rob (2024). What is the Project Management Triangle? Forbes. https://www.forbes.com/advisor/business/project-management-triangle. Accessed 10 December 2024.

Stempel, Jonathan (2024). Lyft earnings report error prompts shareholder lawsuit. Reuters. https://www.reuters.com/legal/lyft-earnings-report-error-prompts-shareholder-lawsuit-2024-03-06. Accessed 30 November 2024.

INDEX

Please note that page numbers referring to Figures are followed by the letter '*f*'

A

accountability, ensuring, 167, 169
see also transparency, ensuring
accounting software, 58
accounts receivable (AR), 83
action titles, 195–6, 198
action(s)
implementation plan, 46, 169, 213–15
insights moving to/ resulting in, 37
none taken following meetings, 29
recommended, 209–10

steps for communicating financials to executives, 39, 46–7
titles in slider headers and charts, 198
turning discussion into, 166–8
ad hoc analysis, 23
adaptation skills for different audiences, 226–7
ADKAR framework, 238–41
ability, 240
awareness, 239
desire, 239
knowledge, 239–40
reinforcement, 240–1

INDEX

advisory function of companies, 7, 8

AI (artificial intelligence), 71–2

analysis of data *see* data analysis

analytics
  descriptive, 94–5, 98, 99, 109
  diagnostic, 94, 98, 99, 109, 110
  predictive, 71, 94, 96–7, 98, 99, 109
  prescriptive, 94, 97–8, 99
  steps for communicating financials to executives, 93, 94, 98
  types, 93–9

argumentation, 137–55
  argument tree, 145*f*
  arguments as art of persuasion, 139–40
  case example of Sarah (Senior Financial Analyst), 153–5
  customer testimonials, 147–8
  decision-making, 153
  examples of interplay between fact, interpretation and argument, 141–2
  expert statements, 146–7
  vs. facts, 138–42
  impact, 152
  industry research, 148–9
  interplay of facts with arguments, 140–2
  presenting only evidence supporting the argument on a slide, 198
  relevance of argument, 151
  selectivity, importance of, 150–2
  selecting appropriate three arguments, 151–2
  simplicity of argument, 152
  supporting recommendations with arguments, 132
  three arguments as ideal, 142–6
  argument tree, 145*f*

to convince
management, 144–6
'magic number of
three' argument,
142–6
psychology behind
number three,
143–4
see also facts
assistants, AI, 71–2
attention
key attention points,
defining *see* insights
(key attention
points)
loss of, 19, 24, 25, 40, 178
pre-attentive attributes,
186, 187–8, 189, 191
span of
and cognitive
functioning, 178
decreasing, 178
factors influencing,
178
short, 19, 99, 101, 178
split-attention effect,
185–6
visual attention test,
examples, 187, 189

see also insights (key
attention points)
audience
adaptation skills for
different audiences,
226–7
attention, loss of, 19, 24,
25, 40
catering to, 85–6
considering what is seen/
experienced by,
87–8, 109
current behaviour,
indicating priorities,
88–9
decisions to be made
by, based on
presentation, 87,
109, 110
differing priorities of, 56
executive, 184
getting to know, 55–6
identifying, 86–7, 109
interviewing senior
stakeholders, 236
likely responses,
considering, 88, 109
management reports,
adapting to, 201

INDEX

audience (*continued*)
matters probably
heard by before
presentation, 89, 109
objective/target
stakeholder,
identifying, 55–7
perspectives of, 57, 90–1
tailoring analysis to, 56–7
thoughts and feelings,
89–90, 109
whether can influence
relevant situation, 84
see also executives;
stakeholders
autonomy, SCARF model,
161–2, 163, 170–1

B
bar charts, 190
BI (business intelligence),
57–8, 71
Big Data, 3
Big Five personality traits,
92
brain
and cognitive ease, 100
cognitive strain, 186
data visualizations,
perception of, 180
charts, 190
images, processing,
74
verbal and visual
information,
processing, 179,
183, 185, 188
Gestalt principles, 188
limbic system, 89–90
making financial
information
"brain-friendly," 183
organizing information
in optimal way, 188
patterns, processing of
information in, 100,
143, 187
pre-attentive attributes,
187
and rule of three, 143,
144
split-attention effect,
185–6
see also attention;
System 1 and 2
thinking
brainstorming solutions,
42, 46
budgets
annual, 110

Index

closing revenue gap to,
109, 111, 153, 154,
155, 170, 172, 173
comparing actuals to, ix,
11, 24, 25, 29, 37,
69–70, 82, 95, 110, 207
control through, 7, 8
5× Why analysis, 125, 126*f*
forecasts, 66, 70
monthly, 110
realistic, 165
resources, 123
revenue below, 110, 172
variances from, 37, 77, 207
see also variances
bullet points, use of, 186
business
changing, 10
growing, 10
results, 9
running, 10
SCQA model, 222–3
business intelligence *see* BI
(business intelligence)

C

case example of Sarah
(Senior Financial
Analyst at Solara
Tech Inc.), 17–18

backing up
recommendations,
153–5
data, struggles with,
76–8
difficulty in
communicating
financials, 28–30
financial status of
information, 172
getting started, 172–3
getting to know
customers, 47–50
key attention points,
172
knowing if something is
a good idea, 172
meetings, 48, 49, 78
potential solutions,
identifying, 132–5
presentations, 170–3
shortcomings
in financial
presentations,
28–30
uncovering root causes
of poor revenue
performance,
108–11
cash flows, negative, 82–3

INDEX

CCOs (Chief Commercial Officers), 50, 56, 85, 108, 109, 118, 155
  implementation process, 169, 171
  management reports, 206, 209, 211
certainty
  99% mindset/need for certainty, 27
  SCARF model, 161, 163, 170
  and uncertainty in financial forecasting, 192
CFOs (Chief Financial Officers), 8, 83
  high-risk internal communications made by, 13
  influence on stock price, 12, 13
  jobs on line in every communication, 13, 14–15
  management system considerations, 14–15

  non-financial matters, involvement in, 15
  struggle to deliver expected value, 14
  whether caring about what is being presented, 83, 84
  work done by, 12–13
change, resistance to *see* resistance to change, anticipating; SCARF model
Chart of Accounts (CoA), 62–3
charts, 29, 36, 192, 199
  bar charts, 190
  colours, using to make easy to read, 200
  complex, 193–4
  junk, removing, 193–4
  multidimensional, avoiding, 194
  pie charts, 190, 191
  pre-attentive attributes, 187
  strategic use of elements in, 187
  swapping tables for, 74
  titles in, 198

two-dimensional, 194
see also slide-making;
visualization, data
Chief Commercial
Officers *see* CCOs
(Chief Commercial
Officers)
Chief Financial Officers
see CFOs (Chief
Financial Officers)
Chief Human Resource
Officers *see* CHRO
(Chief Human
Resource Officers)
Chief Information
Officers *see* CIOs
(Chief Information
Officers)
Chief Marketing Officers
see CMOs (Chief
Marketing Officers)
Chief Operational
Officers *see* COOs
(Chief Operational
Officers)
CHRO (Chief Human
Resource Officer), 83
chunking technique,
143–4

CIOs (Chief Information
Officers), 83, 85
cloud storage, 61
CMOs (Chief Marketing
Officers), 133
CoA *see* Chart of Accounts
(CoA)
cognitive ease, 100
cognitive load, minimizing,
182–3
COGS (cost of goods sold),
116
colour, effective use of, 181,
191–2, 200, 204
common-size analysis *see*
vertical data analysis
communication, financial
courses on executive
communication,
29–30
difficulty in
communicating
financials
successfully *see* poor
quality financial
presentations
framework, need for,
15–16
and influence, 6

INDEX

communication, financial
courses on executive
communication
(*continued*)
intrinsic motivation for,
12–13, 17
investing in increasing
ability to
communicate, 8
reasons for importance
see importance
of financial
communication,
reasons for
storytelling, 23–6
top-down
communication
principle, 38–9
WHY, WHAT and HOW
we communicate,
6–7
WHY and WHAT of,
13
WHY of, 10, 32
see also communication
skills
communication
skills
acquiring, 217–31

adaptation skills for
different audiences,
226–7
business cases, 222–3
first steps
asking the audience,
236
comparison and
feedback, 235–6
mock-up, preparing,
236–7
following the meeting,
230–1
getting to work, 243–4
Golden Rule of Three,
99–101
learning and
development, 234
before the meeting,
228–9
at the meeting, 229–30
practical steps to
improve, 233–47
ability, 240
ADKAR framework,
238–41
awareness, 239
desire to change, 239
first steps, 235–8

implementation and
continuous
improvement, 237–8
knowledge, 239–40
new company culture,
241–3
next steps, 238–41
reinforcement, 240–1
presentation skills,
223–4, 225*f*, 226
SCAQ framework, 218
tips for communication,
99–106
company culture, new, 241–3
comparative analysis, 67, 69
comparison and feedback,
235–6
completeness of
information,
excessive focus on, 25
compliance function of
companies, 7–8, 14
deadlines, 103
control function of
companies, 7, 8, 14
COOs (Chief Operational
Officers), 50, 56, 89
management reports,
207, 209

copilots, AI, 71, 72
correlation analysis, 96,
110
cost considerations
cost advantages, 69
cost centres, 242
cost drivers, 96
cost of goods sold
(COGS), 116
cost–benefit analysis, 98
cost-saving measures,
139, 141
escalating costs, 123
extraordinary cost
variances, 121
horizontal data analysis,
64, 66
implementation process,
165
increased costs, 96, 140
indirect costs, 123
line-by-line cost review,
205
management reports, 205
negative trends, 121
options, presenting, 131
overheads, 116
overruns, 25
in presentations, 24

INDEX

cost considerations
(*continued*)
problem-solving, 123
profit and loss (P&L)
statements, 56
raw materials, 141
reduced costs, 124, 141,
146, 198
relative cost of goods
sold, 68
resources, 123
structures, 139
supplier costs, 139
unexpected costs, 70
variable costs, 25
vertical data analysis, 67,
68
CPOs (Chief People
Officers), 50, 207, 209
credibility, 40
criteria
curating content based
on, 101–4
importance, 102
success, 124
urgency, 102–3
CRM (Customer
Relationship
Management), 58, 78

customer relationship
management *see*
CRM (Customer
Relationship
Management)
customer satisfaction, 9
customer testimonials,
147–8
Customer Value Model, 33
customer-centric approach,
taking, 5, 32, 33–5

D
data, financial
accessing relevant
sources, 57–8
analysis *see* data analysis
case example of Sarah
(Senior Financial
Analyst), 76–8
cleaning, 60–2, 76, 177
combining with
non-financial, 11
complex, 182
conflicting datasets, 60
data-driven
decision-making
framework, 3, 4, 8,
98, 140, 148

entering same information multiple times, 77
essential, highlighting only, 182
extracting, 57–8
extrapolation, horizontal, 66
facilitating decision-making, 3, 4
finding, 177
hard data, 149
inaccurate datasets, 61
integration, 57
integrity, 61, 62
irrelevant, 150
large datasets, 72
linking to CoA, 63
management, mastering of, 59–60
moving from to insights, 36–8
non-numerical facts integrating with, 149
only loosely connected to recommendation, 151
preparation, 59–63

reliability, 61
reporting, 106
selection, 72–5
simplification through vertical analysis, 68
standardization, 68, 69
story in, 36–7
suppliers, 48
visualization *see* visualization, data
see also data analysis; information
data analysis, 57, 63–72, 177
analytical process irrelevant to management, 73–4
defining analytical objective, 63
defining clear purpose/ objective prior to, 52–3
horizontal, 64–6, 77
potential insights, 63
vertical, 66–9
Data Science, 3
databases, 58, 61
deadlines, 103, 164, 169
decimals, reducing, 192

INDEX

decision trees, 97
decision-making
accountability, ensuring, 167, 169
accuracy, 60
argument, decisions following, 153
by audience, 87, 109, 110
avoiding decision paralysis, 166–7
balanced approach to data analysis/ intuition, 89
business leaders wanting more involvement from Finance, 118–19
and change, 162
consistence, 60
criteria, curating content based on, 102
daily load, 19
data-driven, 3, 4, 8, 98, 140, 148
findings aiding, 74
focusing skills, 53, 54, 72
improved, insights and recommendations not automatically leading to, 18, 19, 26

insights for improved decisions, 32, 106
insisting on a decision, 166–8
need for fast decisions by executives, 2, 3, 145, 150, 181
objective/target stakeholder, identifying, 54–5
reliability, 60
solid data, need for, 3, 4
transparency, ensuring, 163, 165
Deming, W. Edwards, 140
descriptive analytics, 94–5, 98, 99, 109
detailed financial presentations, avoiding, 20, 21–3, 40, 185
deviations, 29, 78, 95
budget vs. actual, 82
drivers of, 73
positive or negative, 40
substantial, highlighting, 73
and variances, 69–70
see also budgets; variances

Index

diagnostic analytics, 94, 98, 99, 109, 110
dialogue, 4, 49, 131–2, 135, 158
  sales, 133, 155, 171
  technical, 29
drill-down analysis, 96
dual-coding, 183, 184, 184*f*

E
efficiency
  ambiguity removal, 196
  analysis process, 35, 61, 62
  assessment, vertical analysis, 67–8
  chart junk, removing, 193
  data flows, 238
  financial statements, 63
  gains, realizing, 88–9, 147
  identifying inefficiencies, 68, 70, 125, 135
  improving, 56
  objective, defining, 53
  operational, 103, 104
  presentation of insights, 72
  running of business, 10

System 1 thinking, 180
vertical data analysis, 68, 69
Einstein, Albert, 121–2, 128
empathy, 86–93
ERP (enterprise resource planning), 57, 58, 61
essential and non-essential information, need to separate, 22, 24, 41
  presenting only data that matters, 72–5
  selectivity, importance of, 150–2
Excel *see* Microsoft Excel
executives
  communicating financials to successfully, xi, 6, 12, 16, 17, 31, 46, 51, 239, 243
  see also communication, financial; communication skills; poor quality financial presentations;

261

INDEX

executives (*continued*)
 presentations; steps
 for communicating
 financials to
 executives;
 visualization, data
on data-driven
 decision-making,
 3–4, 119
decreasing tenure, 3
enabling immediate
 understanding,
 facilitating
 decision-making,
 181, 183, 186, 188,
 189, 192, 195
influencing by financial
 professionals, 5–6, 178
lack of expertise in
 financial matters, 2,
 3, 11, 32, 35
lack of time
 considerations, 11,
 19–20, 26, 145, 195
loss of attention, 3, 39,
 178
non-financial data,
 understanding, 11
numbers of meetings
 attended, 19

objectives when
 listening to financial
 professionals, 25
pressures on, 2, 3–4,
 19–20, 26, 177
priorities taken into
 account, 6, 23, 41–2,
 48, 56
steps for communicating
 financials to, 31–50
see also audience;
 communication
 skills;
 communication,
 financial; meetings;
 presentations;
 stakeholders
expert statements, 146–7

F
facts
 vs. arguments, 138–42
 defining, 138–9
 expanding definition
 beyond numbers,
 146–9
 as foundation of trust,
 138–9
 interplay with
 arguments, 140–2

non-numerical,
   integrating
   with financial
   data, 149
and recommendations,
   45
see also argumentation
fairness, SCARF model,
   162–3, 171
Finance
   business leaders
      desiring more
      involvement from,
      in decision-making,
      118–19
   creating impact, 11
   purpose of, 7–10
   value of, 10–12
financial communication
   see communication,
      financial
financial professionals
   intrinsic motivation for,
      12–13, 17
   reporting from, 18
   struggles to
      communicate
      financials *see* poor
      quality financial
      presentations

financial statements
   analysis, 95
   built on logical
      structures, 32
   failure to emphasize the
      important points,
      24–5
   see also profit and loss
      (P&L) statements
financial status of
   information,
   51–78
   accessing relevant data
      sources, 57–8
   analysis of data, 63–72
   audience, considering,
      55–7
   case example of Sarah
      (Senior Financial
      Analyst), 172
   Chart of Accounts
      (CoA), 62–3
   cleaning of data, 60–2
   credibility, 40
   decision in focus, 54–5
   extracting data, 57–8
   identifying entity in
      focus, 53
   master data
      management, 59–60

INDEX

financial status of
  information,
  (*continued*)
moving from
  information to
  insights, 75–6
objective, defining, 52–7
preparation of data,
  59–63
presenting in first
  meeting, 203
presenting only what
  matters, 72–5
selection of data, 72–5
sticking to the facts in a
  presentation, 208
target stakeholder,
  defining, 52–7
technology, using to one's
  advantage, 70–2
timeline in focus, 53–4
variances and deviation,
  69–70
see also data, financial
financials
difficulty in
  communicating *see*
  poor quality financial
  presentations

starting with in a
  presentation, 25
steps for communicating
  to executives, 31–50
5× Why analysis, 125, 126*f*,
  127
focusing skills, 22, 23, 32,
  33, 50
decisions, 53, 54, 72
entity in focus, 53
Golden Rule of Three,
  100, 101
key insights,
  highlighting, 101
timeline in focus, 53–4
forecasts
forecasting models, 96
future performance, 65–6
uncertainty involved in,
  192
see also budgets;
  deviations;
  variances

G
Gestalt principles, 186,
  188–9
Golden Rule of Three,
  99–101

Index

Google Sheets, 61
graphs, 36, 187, 193

H
Head of Sales Channels,
169, 170–1
historical reporting, 98–9
horizontal data analysis,
64–6, 77
see also trend analysis
how-trees, 128, 129, 133,
134*f*, 135

I
impact
communicating with, 6
equation, 4, 5*f*
facts/arguments, 152
Finance creating, 11
financial, 104
high-impact insights, 103
insight x influence =
impact formula, 4–7,
114
of insights, 84
long-term, 102
proving efforts are
making, 9
short-term, 103

implementation process,
46, 169
common understanding,
summarising/
ensuring, 157–8
connections, building,
162
cost considerations, 165
decision-making, 166–8
getting started with,
157–73
high-level plan, in
management report,
213–15
identifying channel
partners, 169–70
options, presenting, 162
paving the way forward,
163–5
project triangle, 164*f*,
165
quality, 165
resistance to change,
anticipating, 16
SCARF model *see*
SCARF model
scope, 165
time, 164–5
see also action(s)

265

INDEX

importance of financial communication, reasons for, 1–16

impact equation, 4, 5*f*

influence, 4–7

insight, 4–7

mounting pressure on executives, 2, 3–4

purpose of finance, 7–10

inconsistent structure, avoiding, 23–6

industry peers, comparisons with, 69

industry research, 148–9

influence

on decision-making, 11

defining, 5

going beyond, 6

insight x influence = impact formula, 4–7, 114

infographic, 181, 184

information, 39–40

aggregating, 73

completeness, excessive focus on, 25

easy to understand, need for, 2, 3–4

essential and non-essential, need to separate, 22, 24, 41, 72–5

selectivity, importance of, 150–2

financial status, 51–78

newsworthy, 81–4

noteworthy, 81–4

organizing for better understanding (Gestalt principles), 188–9

overload, 72

time sensitivity, 103

treating all equally, 24

see also data, financial

insights (key attention points), 79–111

case example of Sarah (Senior Financial Analyst), 172

combining financial and non-financial data, 11

communicating, 99–106

curating content based on criteria, 101–4

decision-making, improving, 32, 106

Index

defining, 5, 11, 80–4
execution, 114, 115
financial status of
  information, 75–6
five-step framework, 79,
  80*f*
generating, 11
high-impact, 103
identifying, 63
insight x influence =
  impact formula, 4–7,
  114
moving from data to, 36–8
moving to
  recommendations,
  106, 108
moving to/resulting in
  action, 37
new information,
  relevant to audience's
  decisions, 80–1
optimal presentation of
  arguments, 176
personality types,
  acknowledging, 91–2
predictive, 65
presenting in second
  meeting, 203
proportional, 67

relevant to stakeholders,
  presenting, 86–93
'So what?' questions, 79,
  82, 86, 98, 105, 106
steps for communicating
  financials to
  executives, 41–2
synthesizing vs.
  summarizing, 104–6,
  107*f*
understanding
  stakeholders'
  perspectives,
  verifying, 90–1
verifying understanding,
  90
see also attention;
  audience;
  recommendations

J
jargon, minimizing, 40, 75
journalist, thinking like,
  31, 42, 105

K
Kahneman, Daniel, 89–90
  Thinking, Fast and Slow,
  180

INDEX

L

Lafley, A. G., Playing to
Win framework, 14
limbic system, 89–90
see also System 1 and 2
thinking
logic trees, 127, 128
Lyft, communication
of earnings
expectations, 13

M

machine learning
algorithms, 71
'magic number of three'
argument *see*
argumentation
management meetings, 78,
111, 153, 216, 227,
238
implementation process,
166, 168, 171
management reports, 30,
82, 201–16, 217
adapting to target
audience, 201
comparing actuals to
budget, ix, 24, 29
condensed, 205

constructive feedback,
214
mock-up of perfect
report, 206–16, 236
standard, 29
structure of, 203–6
Appendices, 205
Page 1 (scope, period
covered, audience,
person preparing
and date of
preparation), 204
Page 2 (financial
status), 204, 207–8
Page 3 (key attention
points), 204, 205,
208–9
Page 4 (recommended
actions), 204, 205,
209–10
Page 5 (significant
arguments), 204,
210–12
Page 6 (risks and
benefits), 204,
212–13
Page 7 (high-level
implementation
plan), 205, 213–15

Page 8 (summary/ next steps), 205, 215–16
summarization and synthesizing, 105–6
trust-building, 202–3
management team members, consultation with, 48–9
market position, 103, 104
Martin, Roger, Playing to Win framework, 14
master data management (MDM) *see* MDM (master data management)
MDM (master data management), 59–60, 76–7
meetings
  brainstorming solutions, 42
  case example of Sarah (Senior Financial Analyst), 48, 49, 78
  communication skills following the meeting, 47, 230–1
  before the meeting, 34–5, 228–9
  at the meeting, 229–30
  debriefs on findings, 41
  discussions falling short of real change, 166
  early finish, 29
  first meeting, use of, 203
  with highest priority stakeholder, 34
  management, 78, 111, 153, 166, 168, 171, 216, 227, 238
  monthly, 22, 37, 39, 50, 111
  no actions taken following, 29
  numbers attended by executives, 19
  presentations given at, 3, 228–31
  presenting a plan, 46
  on profit and loss, example, 22–3
  recommendations, promoting, 45
  second meeting, matters focused on, 203

INDEX

meetings (*continued*)
 validation of solutions
 prior to, 43
 see also presentations
memorability, 100
Microsoft Excel, 61, 62
Minto, Barbara, 7, 31, 223,
 225*f*, 242
moments of
 communication,
 1–2, 32
Monte Carlo simulation,
 97
multidimensional charts,
 avoiding, 194

N
net present value (NPV),
 87

O
OCEAN model,
 personality types, 92,
 93*f*
operational efficiency, 103,
 104
opinions, voicing, 118–19
options, presenting, 43,
 44–5, 130–1, 162

P
partnership programs, 154
past performance,
 understanding, 66
performance evaluation,
 horizontal analysis,
 65
personality types,
 acknowledging, 91–2
persuasion, art of, 139–40
pie charts, 190, 191
plain language, using, 40, 75
Playing to Win framework
 (Lafley and
 Martin), 14
poor quality financial
 presentations, 12, 14,
 17–30
 99% mindset/need for
 certainty, 27
 belief that others know
 best, 27
 case example of Sarah
 (Senior Financial
 Analyst), 28–30
 completeness, excessive
 focus on, 25
 detail, excessive, 20,
 21–3, 40, 185

270

examples of poor quality
communication, 13,
22–3
failure to lead to better
decision-making, 26
financial statements,
failure to emphasize
the important points,
24–5
inconsistent structure,
23–6
lack of time
considerations, 11,
19–20, 26
loss of attention, leading
to, 19, 24, 25, 40
making no apparent
recommendations,
26–8, 113–14
need for improvement,
15, 18, 19, 26
purpose in reviewing, 18
separating the
essential from
the non-essential,
problems with, 22,
24, 41
summarizing, limitations
in, 27–8

Power BI, 58
pre-attentive attributes,
186, 187–8, 189, 191
predictive analytics, 71, 94,
96–7, 98, 99, 109
see also budgets;
forecasts
prescriptive analytics, 94,
97–8, 99
presentations
adapting communication
to audience, 226–7
case example of Sarah
(Senior Financial
Analyst), 170–3
checking-in with
executives prior to,
41–2
concluding by paving the
way forward, 163–5
cost considerations in, 24
data-backed, 58
excessive detail, avoiding,
20, 21–3, 40, 185
impact on executives, 84
presentation skills,
223–4, 225f, 226
rehearsing, 171–2
review of, 16

INDEX

presentations (*continued*)
  SCARF model, applying prior to, 163
  starting with financials, 25
  tailoring to audience's preferences, 92
  use of colour *see* colour, effective use of
  verbal, 185
  visualization of data *see* visualization, data
  see also audience; communication, financial; communication skills; executives; insights (key attention points)
priorities, focus on, 23, 41–2, 48
  differing priorities of audience, 56
problem-solving, structured
  defining the problem, 120, 121–4
  designing the solution, 120, 128–9

disaggregating the problem, 120, 124–8
  5× Why analysis, 125, 126*f*, 127
  symptoms vs. root causes, 124, 125*f*
  why tree, 127*f*
how-trees, 128, 129, 133, 134*f*, 135
leveraging, 120–9
logic trees, 127, 128
options, presenting, 130–1
principles, 119
resources, 123
scope of problem, 122–3
stakeholders, considering, 122
success criteria, 124
why-trees, 127, 128
profit and loss (P&L) statements, 24
cost aspects, 56
example meeting, 22–3
project triangle, 164*f*, 165
prototype (making solution visible), 129–30
Pyramid Principle (Minto), 7, 31, 223, 225*f*, 242

Q
Qlik, 58

R
ratio analysis, 95
real option analysis, 98
recommendations
  anticipating objections, 131–2, 213
  apparent, failure to make, 26–8
  backing up, 153–5
  buy-in and acceptance of, 44, 46, 90, 163–4, 205–6
  data only loosely connected to, 151
  facing resistance when presenting, 44–5
  facts, types of, 45
  making solution visible (prototyping), 129–30
  management reports, 209–10
  moving from insights to, 106, 108
  never just one solution option, 130–1

not automatically leading to improved decision-making, 18, 19, 26
options, presenting, 43, 44–5, 130–1, 162
preparing to make, 111
proactivity, showing, 43
proving benefits of, 45
steps for communicating financials to executives, 39, 42–4
strength of, 151, 152
supporting with arguments, 132
tips for making, 129–32
regression analysis, 97
regulatory deadlines, 103
relatedness, SCARF model, 162, 171
relational database, 61
reporting, 16, 18, 106
  capabilities, 71
  historical, 98–9
  internal financial, 8
  management *see* management reports

INDEX

reporting (*continued*)
monthly, 21
periods, 49
standard package, 22
resistance to change,
anticipating,
158–63
resolution, 113–35
case example of Sarah
(Senior Financial
Analyst), 132–5
daring to have an
opinion, 118–19
distinguishing between
output and outcome,
115–17
leveraging structured
problem-solving,
120–9
defining the problem,
121–4
designing the solution,
128–9
disaggregating the
problem, 124–8
mitigating actions, 213
product profitability
analysis example,
116–17, 118

tips for making a
recommendation *see*
recommendations
resources, 165, 173, 177
allocating, 54, 55, 67,
68–9
misallocating, 125
reallocating, 87, 117,
159, 161
cognitive processing, 185
constraints, 123
and costs, 123
enterprise resource
planning, 57, 58, 61
implementation plan,
223
resource-intensive
products, 68
Sales and Operations,
214
wasting, 122–3
return on investment
(ROI), 87
Rock, David, 159
root cause analysis
challenging, 133
diagnostic analytics,
95–6, 98
identification, 128

missing leads example, 132–3, 172

increasing number of leads, 134

increasing quality of leads, 135

and potential solutions, 132–5

symptoms vs. root causes, 124, 125*f*

uncovering root causes of poor revenue performance, 108–11

rule of three, 143

see also argumentation

S

Sarah (Senior Financial Analyst), case example of *see* case example of Sarah (Senior Financial Analyst at Solara Tech Inc.)

SCARF model, 159–71, 160*f*

applying before presentation, 163

autonomy, 161–2, 163, 170–1

certainty, 161, 163, 170

fairness, 162–3, 171

relatedness, 162, 171

status, 159, 161, 163, 170

scenario analysis, 97

scope

of project, 165

management reports, 204

structured problem-solving, leveraging, 122–3

SCQA (situation, complication, question, answer) framework, 218

benefit case, 222

business cases, 222–3

differences between using/not using, 221

e-mailing using, 220, 221*f*

e-mailing without using, 220

examples, 219–20, 224

implementation plan, 223

from pyramid to presentation mode, 224, 225*f*

SCQA (*continued*)
reporting, 227
risks and assumptions,
222–3
see also communication
skills
screens, use of large
readable fonts, 200
selectivity, importance of,
150–2
see also essential and
non-essential
information, need to
separate
70/20/10 approach to
learning, 234
shortcomings in financial
presentations
see poor quality
financial
presentations
short-termism, 3, 103
slide-making
action titles, using in
header and charts,
198
call-out boxes/bold text
to emphasize critical
data points, 199–200

example of perfect slide,
196, 197*f*
excessive detail, avoiding,
185
one message per slide,
198–9
perfect slide, example of,
196, 197*f*
placing argument in
header, 198
presenting only evidence
supporting the
argument on header,
199
presenting only evidence
supporting the
argument on the
slide, 198
sources, stating, 199
standard slides,
limitations of, 22–3,
50
tips for, 196, 197*f*,
198–200
using action titles in
header and charts,
198
see also visualization,
data

SMART principle, 218
'So what?' questions, 76, 113
  insights, 79, 82, 86, 98, 105, 106
  steps for communicating financials to executives, 37, 38, 42
  see also 'Then what?' questions
Solara Tech Inc. (solar energy systems manufacturer)
  see case example of Sarah (Senior Financial Analyst at Solara Tech Inc.)
split-attention effect, 185–6
spreadsheet software, 61
SQL (Structured Query Language), 61
stakeholders
  highest priority, meetings with, 34
  identifying, 33–4
  interviewing, 236
  mapping, 48
  perspectives, verifying, 90–1

presenting relevant insights to, 86–93
  prioritizing, 34
  and problem-solving, 122
  target, 52–7
status, SCARF model, 159, 161, 163, 170
  see also financial status of information
steps for communicating financials to executives, 31–50
  action, 39, 46–7
  and analytics, 93, 94, 98
  being factual, 40
  case example of Sarah (Senior Financial Analyst), 47–50
  customer-centric approach, taking, 5, 32, 33–5
  data, 36–8
  delivery capacity and sales pipeline example, 37–8
  evidence, 39, 44–6
  excessive detail, avoiding, 20, 21–3, 40, 185

steps for communicating
financials to
executives,
(*continued*)
five-step framework, 31,
32, 38–9, 168, 216,
218, 233, 235, 237,
242
argumentation, 137,
138*f*
financial status of
information, 51, 52*f*
implementation plan,
getting started, 157,
158*f*, 168
insights, 79, 80*f*
resolution, 113, 114*f*
identifying stakeholders,
33–4
information, 39–40
insights, 36–8, 39, 41–2
jargon, minimizing, 40,
75
management team
members,
consultation with,
48–9
needs, understanding,
34–5

prioritizing
stakeholders, 34
recommendations, 39,
42–4
'So what?' questions, 37,
38, 42
'Then what?' questions,
37, 38
top-down
communication
principle, 38–9
validation
phase, 43
stock price, influence of
CFO on, 12, 13
storytelling, 23–6, 182
data, finding story in,
36–7
storyline heading, 226
strategic alignment, 102
structured
problem-solving,
leveraging *see*
problem-solving,
structured
Structured Query
Language *see* SQL
(Structured Query
Language)

summarization
 defining, 105
 limitations in, 27–8
 vs. synthesizing, 104–6, 107*f*
supply chain management tools, 58
synthesizing
 case example of Sarah (Senior Financial Analyst), 111
 defining, 105–6
 vs. summarizing, 104–6, 107*f*
System 1 and 2 thinking
 cognitive load, minimizing, 182–3
 comparing, 180–1
 defining, 89–90
 designing for System 1, 181
 engaging System 2 when necessary, 182

T
Tableau, 58
technology, using to one's advantage, 70–2
'Then what?' questions, 98, 108, 113
 steps for communicating financials to executives, 37, 38
 see also 'So what?' questions
Thorbecke, Johan, 203
time considerations
 deadlines, 103, 164, 169
 executives' lack of time, 11, 19–20, 26, 145
 implementation process, 164–5
 structured problem-solving, leveraging, 123
time sensitivity, 103
time series analysis, 97
timelines, in focus, 53–4
transparency, ensuring, 163, 165
 see also accountability, ensuring
trend analysis, 64, 95
 see also horizontal data analysis
trend identification, 64
trust-building, 202–3

INDEX

U

urgency, evaluating, 102–3

V

value interventions, 9

variance analysis, 69–70, 95, 121

variances, ix, 206
  above an agreed threshold, 205
  actual and budget, between *see* budgets
  CoA, linking financial data to, 63
  critical, coding of, 204
  decomposition, 96
  explaining, 25
  extraordinary cost, 121
  highlighting, 70
  highlighting deviations, 73
  positive or negative, 70
  revenue analysis, 77
  small, 20
  treating all equally, 24
  visibly explaining, 202
  see also budgets; deviations; variance analysis

verbal information,
  presenting along with visuals, 130, 183, 184
  management reports, 219
  and split-attention effect, 185–6
verbal processing channel, 186
vertical data analysis, 66–9
  compared with horizontal, 66
  cost considerations, 67, 68
visualization, data, 175–200
  action headers, 196
  action titles, 195–6, 198
  arrows, 196
  bullet points, 186
  charts *see* charts
  colour, effective use of, 181, 191–2, 200, 204
  decimals, reducing, 192
  decoding key message easily, enabling, 177–9

dual-coding, 183, 184*f*
fonts on screen,
    large and readable,
    200
Gestalt principles, 186,
    188–9
graphs, 36, 187, 193
highlighting main points,
    195
labels, 196
layout, 181
less is more principle,
    193–4
pairing of visuals with
    words, 183–6
pre-attentive attributes,
    186, 187–8
rounding of numbers,
    192–3
shape, 181

split-attention effect,
    185–6
System 1 and 2 thinking
    see System 1 and 2
    thinking
tables compared with
    visuals, 74
tips for improvement,
    189–96
visual appeal, 36, 40, 183
see also slide-making;
    verbal information,
    presenting along
    with visuals

W
why-trees, 127, 128
    see also 5× Why analysis
words, pairing with visuals,
    183–6